FORECASTING METHODS FOR HORSERACING

by Peter May

Raceform

Newbury
Berkshire, England

May, Peter.
    Forecasting methods for horseracing / Peter May

Copyright © Peter May 1998

ISBN 1-901100-31-6

Published by Raceform Ltd.,
Compton, Newbury, Berkshire, England, RG20 6NL.
www.raceform.co.uk

ACKNOWLEDGEMENTS

Firstly I would like to thank my friends and colleagues at Oxford Brookes University for their contributions, direct or indirect, to this book. I would especially like to thank Dr Nigel Crook, an expert in the field of artificial intelligence.

Secondly, I would like to express my gratitude to my family and *racing* friends for their help and contributions, as well as the proof readers John Taylor, Sara Howes and Colin Proffitt. Finally, I would like to thank my wife Sara and daughter Rhianna for their continued support.

Contents

Forecasting Methods: the case of Horseracing

Forecasting the outcome of given situations provides a means of satisfying our natural desire to know the future. In almost every commercial environment there is a need to provide forecasts, from likely crop yields in agriculture to the value of Sterling in the field of finance. The demand for more accurate predictions, coupled with the advances in computer technology, has led to dramatic changes in forecasting methods. It is now possible to supplement traditional statistical forecasting techniques, which have been used for many decades, with rule-based and knowledge-based approaches, which utilise the knowledge gained from human experts in their construction, and machine learning methods in which the computer *learns* from available examples without significant human intervention. This book examines the application of these forecasting methods to the domain of horseracing in Great Britain with the aim of producing a range of techniques which can be used to forecast the results of horseraces.

Forecasting

Forecasting concerns the relating of an outcome to a specific set of circumstances, a 'conjectural estimate of something future' according to the Concise Oxford Dictionary. Humans make many forecasts, or predictions, every day, whether in regard to the likely position of an oncoming vehicle, or the possible result of a sporting event. However, whilst the latter would be unanimously accepted as a forecast, the former would not necessarily be viewed as such. This illustrates two facts: the high degree of diversity associated with forecasting techniques and the importance of this deductive process. The diverse nature of forecasting results from the many different approaches employed in different situations. For example, the fact that the sun always rises in the east, and can be predicted as doing so, can be explained by the laws of planetary motion. However, a knowledge of this theory is not the only basis on which the prediction could be made. For instance, someone who had seen the sun rise in the east for the previous 25 years might also conclude, with as much certainty as the physicist, that the sun will rise in the east tomorrow. These two approaches could hardly be more diverse, however both are valid methods and generate equally accurate predictions. The fact that we devote so much time to forecasting is evidence of its importance, and, furthermore, the way we make our predictions has a bearing on our view of events. Casti[1] asserts in the book *Searching For Certainty* that 'making sense of the things we see and predicting the future course of events have always played an essential role in the formation of each individual's world view'. In essence, forecasting is part of our lives and our ability to make accurate predictions is essential to our survival.

Sporting events, especially horse and greyhound racing, are designed to encourage the public to form an opinion about the event and to express this opinion in the form of a bet. After all without betting neither of these two sports would exist. However, unlike the Lottery and other completely random numbers games, where attempting to forecast the outcome is a pointless task, horseracing poses the race analyst with a challenge that can vary in terms of complexity from the (apparently) trivial to a level commensurate with the most testing *Times* crossword.

It is interesting to note that this level of complexity, although a product of the task itself, is also linked to the analyst's knowledge of racing. To the novice racegoer selecting the probable winner from a field of 24 runners is simply a matter of identifying a well-known jockey or appealing name. To the experienced race bettor such a race may take hours of intensive form study before a conclusion is reached, unfortunately, with no guarantee that this painstaking work will yield a more accurate prediction than the former approach for a single race. Whichever approach you choose, the horseracing problem offers a challenge worthy of our best efforts.

The Horseracing Problem

Thoroughbred horseracing in Great Britain has been extremely well documented for many years. Records still exist detailing the very first organised horseraces, such as the Newmarket Town Plate in which King Charles II was successful in 1671. Consequently, a wealth of information is available to the race analyst, concerning all races and the horses which compete. The historical records include the peculiarities of each race track, whether right or left handed, undulating or flat. For each horse, all previous race details including times, race distances, course conditions and race commentary, together with the animal's pedigree are documented. Jockey and trainer statistics are also available indicating success rates by several variables including track and race type. The fact that racing is so well documented is helpful to the race analyst providing the basic information with which to work.

Although the availability of a large volume of data is advantageous for modelling purposes, the level of information relating to each horse in a race is extremely detailed which severely complicates the task of generating workable systems. Discussion of race analysis methods with recognised racing experts suggests that this level of detail, coupled with a lack of structured approaches to race analysis, has resulted in wide disagreement between the experts regarding optimal solution methods. Although there is general agreement between the experts in the identification of horses with either very high, or very low, probabilities of success, there is considerable disagreement for less well defined runners. Interestingly, these problems mirror those found when developing computerised methods for other prediction problems, such as assessing mortgage applications[2].

A second problem with the horseracing domain is the competition between the runners in a single race. A horse may possess outstanding winning credentials, but the likelihood of its success is also dependent on the abilities of the other runners in the race. This comparison between the animals is a problem even the experts find difficult to handle. For example, a well-known race analyst discussing selection techniques commented: 'and now the guessing starts' when faced with comparing several animals with similar credentials. This competitive element must be considered in any horserace forecasting model in both the output of the system and in the data used to construct the model.

In addition to the vast number of example cases, a major characteristic of the data is the high level of uncertainty associated with many of the components used in the modelling process. This uncertainty is due to the methods used to determine the attributes of the animals on which the forecasts are made. Whilst accuracy is possible with respect to variables such as age, others are subject to measurement error, and some rely totally on opinion. This, naturally, increases the complexity of any modelling procedure. Furthermore, in some cases data will be missing, and to make matters more complicated, a high degree of inter-correlation can exist between the variables. Thus the best jockeys tend to ride for the most successful stables and owners, an important consideration which should certainly not be overlooked, especially when constructing betting systems.

So, we are faced with a complex problem, which although well-documented, comprises missing and uncertain data, complex inter-relationships and an element of within race competition. But it is not an insurmountable problem, and a range of techniques exist to provide a solution.

Intelligent Systems

Many computer systems have been developed that are labelled intelligent. For instance, chess programs are now capable of beating even the very best players. However, any assessment of machine intelligence is dependent upon the definition of the word *intelligent*. Sharkey and Brown[3] argue that, in the main, programmed solutions simply reflect, but do not possess, the intelligence of a human. Since the programs do not produce the solution method themselves they cannot be thought of as intelligent. Other definitions simply require the system to exhibit a level of *understanding* to be labelled intelligent. Understanding implies a depth of knowledge about a specific issue from which, given a reasoning strategy, a conclusion or explanation may be derived. This is where conventional programs and systems categorised as *artificial intelligence* differ. Traditional systems are generally algorithmic: each instruction is performed in an order determined by the program code and they do not exhibit any apparent understanding of the problem. In contrast, some artificial intelligence systems are not constrained by rigid algorithms that dictate the order in which the instructions are performed, and they are able to demonstrate useful reasoning strategies, thereby exhibiting an apparent knowledge of the domain.

Forecasting Methods

Three different forecasting approaches using the ideas and theories of artificial intelligence are examined in this book: rule-based methods, knowledge-based systems and connectionist approaches. Of these methods, the first two, rule-based and knowledge-based techniques are already widely used by race analysts. However, connectionist systems have so far been all but ignored.

As the name suggests, rule-based methods rely on the formulation of rules on which the prediction is based. In horseracing this type of selection method is also referred to as a *system*. Systems provide the bettor with a rigid set of rules to apply to each race in order to determine whether a bet should, or should not, be made. The rules normally take the following form:

> *if   Condition A is true*
> *and Condition B is true*
> *then bet*

In this example, the bettor needs to determine whether the two conditions, A and B, are met, if so the bet should be placed. Complex systems have large rules with many antecedents which need to be satisfied such as in the following rule which is designed for American flat racing[4]:

> *if   the horse has run within the last 15 days*
> *and latest race distance = today's race distance ± 220 yds*
> *and the horse led coming into the home straight in last race*
> *and the horse won its last race by at least 1½ lengths*
> *then bet*

However, their precise and unambiguous form means that even complex rules can be applied without too much difficulty. An investigation of plausible horseracing systems is given in Chapter 5.

Systems offer an easy-to-apply solution to the horseracing problem which is particularly appropriate if the bettor does not have sufficient time to assess each race. Knowledge-based methods, on the other hand, are in general more time-consuming to operate, but offer a more detailed and analytical approach. In a knowledge-based approach the race analyst assesses each horse in the race using a set of predetermined factors considered to provide a basis for discriminating between potential winners and losers. These critical factors form the credentials of each runner in the race, and include its ability based on form or time and the suitability of the race conditions. The difficult part of this approach is combining the factors into a single measure to facilitate comparison of the runners. However, several ways of combining these critical factors have been developed for other applications and these methods are discussed and evaluated in Chapter 6.

The third forecasting technique covered in this book concerns connectionist systems, and specifically the use of artificial neural networks. Artificial neural networks[†] have been defined to be intricate systems of simple units which dynamically adapt to their environments[5], and they offer a radically different approach to processing data from traditional programmed systems. Neural networks comprise a number of interconnected processing elements (nodes) which are analogous to a biological neuron. Numerical weights are associated with the links (connections) between the nodes, which, essentially, constitute the *knowledge* of the system. These weights are derived during a period of *training*, where the system is repeatedly presented with a set of examples until some predetermined convergence criterion is achieved. Hence the system is deemed to learn automatically from the data without instruction from the programmer. Whereas knowledge-based systems model an idealisation of the physical situation as perceived by experts, artificial neural networks model *real* events.

The concept learned by a neural network is represented by the architecture of the system and its numerical weights. A concept is, therefore, often distributed across many node activations, with these nodes also representing parts of other concepts. This approach has advantages when representing imprecise relationships. In fact, Kandel[6] states that 'most real-world problems are too complex and too imprecise to lend themselves to solution by methods based on symbolic manipulation'. In this context *symbolic* refers to knowledge-based approaches utilising rules to represent concepts.

Clearly, neural networks seem appropriate to the horseracing problem. Since they do not rely on existing theory and knowledge, the neural network solution will be unique in terms of its development, resulting in alternative methods of selection which exploit any inaccuracies in currently held beliefs pertaining to traditional race analysis. Neural networks are simple to

---

[†] In the remainder of this text, the terms *neural networks* and *networks* will both refer to artificial neural networks.

implement, and once trained, are quick to execute which means that many races can be analysed in a few seconds. Furthermore, the networks can be tailored to suit the bettor's requirements by modifying the training data. For example, if required the neural networks can be trained with respect to a specific race type, price band (i.e. short priced or long priced animals) or a single trainer. Neural networks can thus be employed in a data mining role identifying certain characteristics to aid the selection process. The applicability of neural networks to the horseracing problem is examined in Chapter 7.

Data Processing

Although neural networks, like other forecasting systems, can be used to map raw input data directly to the required outputs, for non-trivial applications it is often necessary to transform, or pre-process, the input data into a new representation. Except for very simple problems, using raw data as inputs to the model will usually result in poor forecasting performance. Furthermore, it may also be necessary to transform the output from the models, known as post-processing, to an acceptable form. The complete process is presented schematically in figure 1.1. For the horseracing problem, post-processing entails transforming the outputs into degrees of belief (probabilities of success) and ultimately into odds since this is the normal way of expressing chance in this domain. This is discussed in detail in Chapter 4.

The choice of data pre-processing method(s) is one of the most significant

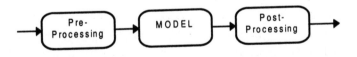

Figure 1.1: Pre- and post-processing

decisions in the model building process and it can have a great impact on the performance of the model. Data pre-processing can take many forms, from simple linear transformations to more complex feature extraction. Pre-processing can also introduce prior knowledge into the model as well as providing a means for handling missing data. As an example consider figure 1.2. When presented with these two patterns the aim of the system is to discriminate between the 'W' and the 'L'. A sample of similar letters would be provided for building the model which would then be tested on new examples.

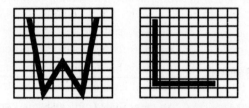

Figure 1.2: Classification patterns

Each letter occupies a subset of the squares on the 10x10 grid. Therefore it would be possible to use each square (or pixel) as an input to the system, with a *used* pixel represented by a one and a blank pixel represented by a zero. Naturally, the system would need to be capable of handling 100 inputs, given the size of the grid. While it would be possible for a neural network, trained on the sample patterns, to classify each correctly, such a system would not, however, be guaranteed to classify new (different) patterns very well. In other words it might not *generalise* well. Generalisation is naturally of great importance in classification and forecasting systems where the aim is to generate statistical models of the data rather than systems which merely memorise historical patterns. As an example, a new pattern could consist of a very small 'W' located in the lower left quarter of the grid. To the human eye the letter is clearly a 'W', however, to the system the arrangement could be meaningless. One possible solution is to extract features from the training data to use in the model. For this example these features could refer to the angle the lines of the letters intersect some defined axes. A (near) horizontal line would then indicate the letter 'L'. A second feature may relate the length of the lines to each other generating a set of ratios which could form another input to the model. Given this information the model is more likely to generalise well to previously unseen patterns.

Another advantage with feature extraction is the reduction in dimensionality which normally accompanies such an operation. For instance in the character classification problem discussed above 100 inputs would be required to represent the raw data. As the number of dimensions increases the volume of historical data required to build the model also increases. Increasing dimensionality rapidly leads to sparse data sets and, as a result, poor input-output mappings. For the horseracing problem a great deal of pre-processing is required. The majority of the data is included in race results and hence needs conversion into an acceptable form. Intermediate conclusions about the animal's likes and dislikes (i.e. suitable race distance) can be gleaned from these results and used as inputs to the model as opposed to the complete race result. Furthermore, it is possible to include prior knowledge in the form of the indicators to the general level of ability of the horse (i.e. a rating) or previous success rates of the trainer or jockey (i.e. classifying the experienced jockeys from the less experienced riders). Methods for pre-processing the horseracing data using feature extraction, inclusion of prior knowledge, and techniques for handling missing data are discussed in Chapter 3.

Objectives

The primary aim of this book is to demonstrate how techniques taken from the field of artificial intelligence can be used to generate forecasting methods for the horseracing problem. Although three, simple, rule-based systems that identify good betting opportunities are presented in Chapter 5, the main focus of this text concerns more complex, computer-based, forecasting methods. Consequently, a knowledge of computer programming and access to a computer is considered beneficial, although a version of the knowledge-based approach could be implemented using a spreadsheet. Apart from the rule-based systems, this text does not include ready-to-use methods, instead it provides a discussion of techniques which are applicable to the horseracing domain and illustrates how these techniques can be combined into forecasting systems. Hopefully the reader will be able to recreate the methods presented, and more importantly, generate new, unique, forecasting systems that produce even more impressive results by constructing more detailed approaches by using the theories expounded in this text. To assist with the development of neural network approaches, a back-propagation algorithm is given in the appendix which can be easily implemented in any programming language. Alternatively, a basic neural network simulation program, details of which are given in appendix A4, which can be used to train small neural network applications can be downloaded from the internet.

References

[1] *Searching For Certainty - what science can know about the future*, by J. L. Casti, Scribners, London, England, 1992.

[2] *An Application of a Multiple Neural Network Learning System to Emulation of Mortgage Underwriting Judgements*, by E. Collins, S. Ghosh and C. L. Scofield, in *IEEE International Conference on Neural Networks*, San Diego, CA, II, pp459-466, 1988.

[3] *Why Artificial Intelligence needs an Empirical Foundation,* by N. E. Sharkey and G. D. A. Brown, in Artificial Intelligence: Principles and Applications, M. Yazdani (ed.), pp267-293, 1986.

[4] *Scientific Handicapping: Tested Ways to Win at the Track,* by I. S. Cohen and G. D. Stephens, Prentice-Hall, Englewood Cliffs, N.J. 1963.

[5] *Connectionism and the Mind: Introduction to Parallel Processing in Networks*, by A. Bechtel and A. Abrahamsen, Oxford, England: Blackwell, 1991.

[6] *Hybrid Architectures for Intelligent Systems*, by A. Kandel, CRCP, London, May 1992.

2

Background Information: Horseracing and Betting

This chapter details the basic information associated with horseracing and betting in Great Britain. The first section covers general information about horseracing including the structure of British races. The differences between handicap and non-handicap races are examined together with other key race types as well as a brief summary defining the going. The second part of the chapter concerns betting. Various forms of bets are discussed with comparisons between the profitability of betting at starting price compared to the Tote pool betting system.

Races and Racecourses

In Great Britain the turf flat racing season starts in late March and ends in early November. This has been the case for many years, though in 1989 the racing programme was supplemented by *all weather* racing, and flat racing now runs through all twelve months of the year. However, it is turf flat racing that is considered in this text.

Racecourses

In 1997 there were 59 racecourses in Great Britain, and more than half of these shared the 5,500 (approximately) scheduled flat races (some courses only stage jump racing). The historical origins of many of the racecourses in this country have resulted in a great diversity of track configurations. For example, Chester racecourse is an almost circular course of approximately one mile in length, as against the 2½ mile Newmarket course on which the horses only make one turn and can race over a straight 1¼ mile of ground. Such wide variations in track shape mean that almost any horse should be suited by at least one course. For instance, according to the Official Formbook[1], sharp-actioned horses are usually suited by Chester whilst the long-striding animal would be better raced at Newmarket.

Courses also vary with respect to the direction in which the horses race: left handed, right handed or, in the case of races exceeding a mile at Windsor, in a figure of eight. Some horses perform better when racing in a particular direction (i.e. left-handed, or right-handed) although this tends to be more relevant for jumps racing where the direction of the course can have a significant effect on the quality of an animal's jumping. Whilst some courses place little emphasis on stamina, as at tracks where the horses tend to run downhill, others can be extremely stiff with a gradual rise in the level of the ground to the finish. For example, the 5 furlong (1 furlong = ⅛ mile) course at Epsom takes approximately 55 seconds to complete, in contrast to the sprint course at Beverley over an equivalent distance which takes on average 62 seconds, almost 13% longer. This significant difference in time is accounted for by the fact that at Epsom the horses race downhill, whereas at Beverley the sprint course rises throughout placing a greater emphasis on stamina.

The Horses

The five and a half thousand races can be categorised in several different ways, one of the most convenient of which is age of the horses. Two-year-old horses (juveniles) do not start racing until the start of the turf season in late March. Although they would be classified as two years old on 1 January, and could in theory race in all weather contests, this additional three months gives them a little more time for physical development. Approximately one quarter of all races are restricted to juvenile horses. Non-juveniles, those of three years and upwards (horses can race until 11 or 12 years old, however few compete in flat races beyond the age of nine), contest the remaining races and are eligible to race throughout the year. This age distinction is very important in flat racing. Only a handful of races each year allow juveniles to compete against older horses, and these two age groups can, therefore, be analysed entirely independently.

Race Types

An alternative classification can be made by considering the type of race. Roughly half of all races are handicap events (known as nurseries if confined to two-year-old horses only). The main difference between handicap races and non-handicaps is that in the case of the former each horse is assigned a different weight to carry (made up of the jockey, saddle, and additional weight added to the weight cloth) by a team of handicappers employed by the British Horseracing Board (BHB). The aim of this artificial handicapping is to give all horses the same chance of winning by penalising the better animals by giving them more weight to carry.

Once qualified for a handicap race, a horse is assigned a handicap mark by the BHB handicappers. This mark is equivalent to a form rating (see next chapter) and is a convenient way of expressing the ability of one horse relative to another. Handicap marks are expressed in pounds, therefore if two three-year-old colts were rated 104 and 108, the latter could be said to be 4 pounds superior to the former, and in a handicap race would carry 4 pounds more weight.

Handicap ratings are adjusted after each race, with the mark of the winner increased on most occasions, and those of horses thought to be too high in the handicap, based on race performance, being reduced. The basis of the handicap adjustments is the distance, in horse lengths, between the horses at the finish of a race, converted to pounds (weight) using a scale based on the race distance. This linear scale can be approximated by the following formula:

$$\text{pounds (weight)} = \frac{\text{distance beaten in lengths} \times 15}{\text{race distance (f)}}$$

Thus if horse A beats horse B by 2 lengths in a 5 furlong race (both carrying the same weight) the superiority in pounds would be estimated at approximately 6lbs (i.e. 2 x 15 / 5). For an equivalent distance between the horses in a 12 furlong race the superiority would be 2½lbs. This conversion is given in tabular form in figure 2.1.

Race distance (f)	5f	6f	7f	8f	10f	12f	14f
pounds per length	3	2.5	2.1	1.9	1.5	1.2	1.1

Figure 2.1: Distance to weight conversion

This conversion provides a basis for calculating the weight adjustments, but the final weight rise/reduction is determined by the handicapper and can vary substantially from race to race depending on the handicapper's assessment of the differences in ability between the runners. For example, although a horse may win by only 1 length, the manner of the victory may result in the handicapper basing its future rating on a win equivalent to, say, 4 lengths. This can give rise to disagreements between the handicappers and the trainers who feel their horses have been harshly treated.

It is important to remember that the ratings do not determine the amount of weight to be carried, just the weight one horse will carry relative to another. It would be possible for two horses to be allotted 7st 10lbs and 8st 0lbs in one race, and 8st 11lbs and 9st 1lb in another race on the same day. The absolute weight carried is determined by the rating of the highest rated horse in the race. In these two hypothetical races, the top rated horse in the first race would be rated higher than the top rated horse in the second race, by fifteen pounds, in fact.

This is an important distinction to make, and it is imperative to remember that a horse carrying 9st 7lbs, for instance, is not necessarily badly handicapped, and an animal set to carry 7st 10lbs is not guaranteed to be well handicapped. The weight carried by a horse simply reflects the overall strength of the race. The fact that a flat handicapper is set to carry 10st is no reason to assume it cannot win.

Naturally, a system that penalises the better animals is open to abuse. Horses that are considered to be too high in the handicap ratings by their trainers or owners may be raced with the intention of reducing this rating as opposed to winning the race. For the owner or trainer of a horse to tell the jockey to prevent the horse from running to its best ability is in breach of the rules of racing. And if a jockey is thought to have *stopped* a horse both the trainer and jockey can be fined and/or suspended. However, there are legal ways of reducing the animal's handicap mark. For instance, running the horse in a race over an unsuitable distance, or on unsuitable going will usually result in defeat and possibly a reduction in the handicap mark. Consequently, handicap races need additional scrutiny before a bet is placed compared to, say, prestigious pattern races where, apart from the pacemakers, all of the horses are running to win.

Although the handicaps/non-handicaps distinction is the most significant, there are several other race types within each of these categories. All races are classified on a scale from A to G (see figure 2.2) which, essentially, relates to the level of prize-money. Grade A races offer the highest levels of prize-money and hence attract the best horses. The average level of prize-money decreases the further down the scale a race is classified, therefore the races are designated as grade G offer the lowest level of prize-money.

Race Type	Race Grade	Prize-money	Conditions, in brief
Group I	A	£70,000-£500,000	*The best races; non-handicaps*
Group II	A	£20,000-£80,000	*Top quality non-handicaps*
Group III	A	£15,000-£45,000	*Good non-handicaps*
Listed	A	£9,000-£30,000	*High standard of horse, some handicaps*
Stakes/ Conditions	B-F	£1,500-£30,000	*Non-handicaps*
Maidens	D-G	£1,500-£15,000	*For horses which have not previously won a race*
Claimers	D-G	£1,200-£4,000	*Each horse can be claimed for the value set by the owner which determines the amount of weight to be carried*
Sellers	E-G	£1,200-£11,000	*Races where the winner is auctioned*
Handicaps	A-G	£1,500-£110,000	*Races where the amount of weight carried is determined by the BHB handicapper*

Figure 2.2: Race types, grades and prize-money

Group I events together with Group II, Group III and Listed events constitute *pattern* races. All pattern races are designated as grade A. These contests naturally attract the best horses and are, in general, non-handicap races except for a few Listed races. The Classics, namely the 1,000 Guineas,

2,000 Guineas, The Derby, The Oaks and The St Leger, are all Group I races.

Other important race types are maiden, claiming and selling races. Only horses which have never won a race of any type can contest maiden races. Basically these races provide a learning ground for horses, allowing them to gain experience against other relatively inexperienced animals. Claiming races are generally contested by moderate animals. Each horse is assigned a value by its owner and this value determines the amount of weight it has to carry. However, after the race the horse may be claimed by another owner for this price. Although setting the value of a horse too low improves its chance of winning by reducing the amount of weight is must carry, it also increases the likelihood of the horse being claimed. Selling races are generally the poorest level of racing in terms of the ability possessed by the runners. At the end of each selling race the winner is auctioned, therefore the winning owner may lose the horse. All of these three race types can be run as non-handicaps or handicaps.

It is an interesting anomaly that of all races, selling events attract the lowest levels of prize-money, however, in order for a winning owner of a seller to retain his/her horse it is necessary for the horse to be bought-in at the auction. This can cost the owner up to 50% of the auction price. Consequently the chance of the owner making a financial gain from this race type is comparatively slim, since if the horse wins the prize-money is poor, and further to this there is the chance of either losing the horse at auction or being required to pay a substantial amount to retain the animal. It is not surprising therefore that these races have a high degree of unpredictability since horses may be running for reasons other than to win (i.e. to reduce their handicap marks). If an animal of modest ability is considered too high in the handicap by the owner/trainer its failure to win several selling races would result in a decrease in its handicap mark thus making its return to non-selling handicap races a more viable option.

Other speciality race types include apprentices' races, restricted to jockeys classified as apprentices, ladies' races and amateur races which are self explanatory. The remaining non-handicap races are referred to as conditions (or stakes) races. These provide a stepping stone for horses just out of maiden company but, as yet, considered too inexperienced for pattern events or handicaps.

Many races have age restrictions in their conditions, for example all of the Classics are restricted to three-year-old horses only. A weight-for-age allowance is introduced in races which allow horses of differing ages to compete. The aim of this allowance is to enable the younger animals to compete on level terms with their mature opponents. The table of weight-for-age allowances is given in appendix A1 and it can be seen that the allowances are dependent on age, race distance and time of year. On 20 May a three-year-old horse would receive a weight allowance of 14lbs from an older horse in a 1¼ mile race, however this allowance reduces to just 4lbs by the end of November illustrating the increased maturity in the younger horse. Along the same lines, when fillies compete against colts, or geldings, they receive a weight allowance of 5lbs, in addition to any weight-for-age allowance.

There is one further complication concerning race conditions that needs explaining. For non-handicap events some horses will be required to carry penalties (i.e. additional weight). The level of these penalties is dictated by the conditions of the race, but will normally take the form of a 5, 6, or 7lbs weight increase. Penalties are incurred by horses which have previously won races. Although it appears anomalous to introduce artificial handicapping into supposedly non-handicaps when there already exists a race classification to cater for the varying abilities of the horses, the fact that the penalty is not based on the ability of the horse but the value of the race the horse won seems absurd. Consequently, it is not necessarily the best horse which wins non-handicaps, since a penalty weight could result in an inferior animal winning. In addition, some races will contain previous winners with different penalties (i.e. penalties gained from winning races of different values), with an inferior horse expected to carry more weight than a more highly regarded opponent. Similarly there would be a weight difference between two animals who finished first and second in a previous race, separated by inches. Although there appears to be no positive reason for introducing a penalty system such as this, especially one which is not based on ability, it has been in place for several years and is not expected to be replaced. At least Group I races are not subject to artificial handicapping, therefore in the vast majority of cases the winner can be considered to be the best horse in the race.

Race Distances

Races may also be categorised by distance. Races over 5 and 6 furlongs are known as sprints, whilst those of over 14f (1¾ miles) are referred to as stamina races. The frequency distribution of all races by race distance is given in figure 2.3.

Race Distance (f)	5-6	7-9	10-13	14+
Percentage of Races	31.0	36.7	25.0	7.2

Figure 2.3: Proportion of races by distance

Figure 2.3 refers to all races, however the distribution is very different for juveniles (two year old horses). As mentioned earlier, two-year-olds are far from fully mature (a horse needs to reach the age of four before it can be said to be fully mature), therefore they tend to run almost exclusively in races of a mile or less. In fact, almost 63% of juvenile races are sprints (5-6 furlongs) and only just over 1% of races exceed a mile. Due to the increasing physical development of two-year-olds during the season the maximum race distance in which they can race increases from 5 furlongs in March and April to 10 furlongs in September.

Ground Conditions

Due to Britain's unpredictable weather, and the fact that the majority of races are run on turf, the underfoot conditions on which the horses race (the *going*) can vary from meeting to meeting, or even day to day. The going is classified in seven categories: Hard (the driest, firmest ground), Firm, Good to Firm, Good, Good to Soft, Soft and Heavy (the wettest, softest ground). There are a further two classifications for all weather surfaces: Fibresand and Equitrack. The all weather tracks at Southwell and Wolverhampton are constructed from Fibresand, whereas the artificial surface at Lingfield is an Equitrack surface.

Since, at present, there is no standard method for measuring the going, unlike the penetrometer in France (though this is being tested at some racecourses this year), the best guide to the state of the ground, after racing, is the race times. Although this is of little benefit to the race analyst needing to know the going prior to racing, it does help make sense of previous race results.

The going can have a significant effect on the result of any race. Soft or heavy ground places a greater emphasis on the stamina of the runners with the races taking longer to run thus improving the chances of the *slower* horses. For example, consider figure 2.4. This graph presents the average race times by the officially recorded going for 12 furlong races.

Average Race Times by Going for 12 Furlong Races

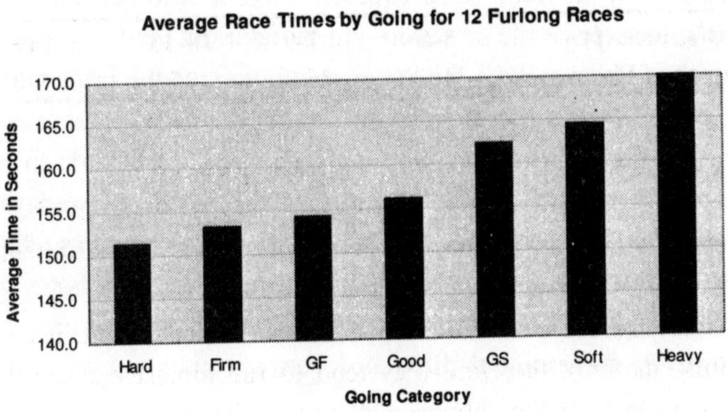

Figure 2.4: Race times by going

From figure 2.4 the effect of different states of ground is immediately apparent. In fact, heavy going increases the race time by 12% compared with hard ground, which is equivalent to almost 1½ furlongs in terms of race distance.

Another important aspect of the going is that it can vary across the width of a racecourse, or between tracks on a single course, such as a straight 5 furlong sprint track compared to the round course. Differences in going at a course can be accounted for by several factors, most usually drainage, watering methods and the configuration of the course. This variability in the course going is of considerable importance when analysing a race and can be used to the bettors' advantage (see section on the *Effect of the Draw* in Chapter 3).

Betting

In Great Britain the betting public can choose between betting with bookmakers or with the Tote. For off-course bettors, the prices offered by the on-course bookmakers are relayed back to the betting offices to allow the punters to take the available price. When the race starts the prices currently on offer at the course are assessed and the average for each horse is returned as its *starting price*. The Tote offers an alternative to conventional bookmakers with prices governed by a pool betting system. The dividend returned to the punter is therefore dependent on the number of winning bets and the total size of the pool. Consequently, anyone who bets on the Tote will not know what price the selection will be returned until after the race. With conventional bookmakers the bettor is able to take the price currently on offer and thus knows the possible return. Historically, there existed a clear distinction between the Tote and conventional bookmakers, in recent years, though, this division has become less well-defined. Nowadays it is possible to bet with the Tote through most off-course bookmakers using the Tote Direct facility (a computer linked to the main Tote machines which control the betting pool), and in all Tote offices it is possible to take boards prices. However, the essential difference between pool and price betting remains.

This choice of betting does come at a cost though, namely an underfunded racing industry. All profits made by the Tote are invested in the horseracing industry i.e. providing prize-money and subsidising racecourses. However, the bookmakers only contribute the levy percentage to racing. This levy of 1.75% is charged together with government tax, on each bet placed off-course (on-course betting is at present *tax* free). It is collected by the bookmakers and then passed on to the racing authorities. Consequently, bookmakers make no direct contribution from profits to racing. However, they do play a vital role with regard to the marketing and promotion of horseracing, and contribute money through race sponsorship. Many commentators have suggested that off-course betting should be restricted to just the Tote in an effort to increase prize-money, reduce the high admission charges at race tracks and improve the general level of facilities provided at the courses. However, this would have the result of decreased competition in the betting market which could result in a poorer deal for the off-course punter.

A further objection to an off-course Tote monopoly concerns the restrictive nature of such a policy. In France, where a Tote monopoly exists, the betting public can only place pool bets. Consequently, they cannot take early prices on the day's racing nor boards prices a few minutes before each race. Pool only betting imposes a severe limitation on the punter. However, it would be possible to restrict all off-course betting offices to Tote ownership but to retain on-course bookmakers as in Australia. In Australia there is a Tote monopoly off-course but on-course boards bookmakers still trade. Therefore, on-course punters are able to take prices as in this country but off-course punters can only place pool bets. However, in such circumstances (Tote ownership of all off-course offices with bookmakers allowed to trade on course), prices could theoretically still be relayed from the track, and early morning prices and ante post prices would still be made available by the Tote thus removing the restriction of pool only betting off-course. The advantage with this approach would be the increased money available to the racing industry and possibly reduced contribution from punters via the levy. The drawback though would be reduced competition no doubt resulting in fewer opportunities for punters to make money. One final point on the possibility of an off-course Tote monopoly is that at present 70-80% of all bets are placed at starting price (*source: William Hill Bookmakers*). In effect, the punters are unaware of the price the horse they have backed will return as in the case of Tote betting. This apparent popularity of starting price betting is not necessarily completely from punters' choice since at present unless the bettor is in the betting office just before the race starts he/she is unable to place any bet other than at starting price. Although early price races are available (i.e. races on which the bookmakers offer prices from the morning onwards) these are very few in number accounting for about 30% of races the vast majority of which are handicaps.

From a betting point of view the combination of both Tote and conventional bookmakers offers the best possible scenario for bettors since it provides the widest possible range of facilities.

Win and Each Way Betting

Win betting is the most popular form of betting in Britain. In fact, most boards bookmakers on-course will only accept straight win bets. As far as the punter is concerned, a selection is made and the win bet placed whether at a given price or starting price. If the horse wins the return is easily calculated by multiplying the stake by the price and then adding the original stake to the total (providing the tax has already been paid). Consequently, a £5.00 win bet (tax paid) placed on a $^6/_5$ winner returns £6.00 plus the £5.00

stake. With the current level of tax at 9% the total outlay (off-course) is £5.45 with a return of £11.00, yielding a profit of £5.55. The tax can also be gambled, though. It is possible to place the bet without paying the tax, but should the horse win the tax is applied to the total return. Using the same example, the total outlay is £5.00, and the return is £11.00 less 9% tax, specifically £10.01. The profit is therefore £5.01.

Clearly, there is a difference in the level of return. So, is it better to pay the tax on the stake (tax paid) or on the return? The answer depends on whether you expect to win or not. If you expect to make a long-term profit from your bets it is better to pay the tax on the stake. However, if, being realistic, you know that in all probability you will lose in the long run it's better to pay the tax on the total return.

Each way betting is a popular alternative to straight win betting. An each way bet comprises two parts: a win bet and a place bet, with a £5.00 each way tax paid bet (£10.90 staked) divided into £5.00 win and £5.00 place. If the horse is successful the win part of the bet is settled as a normal straight win bet, with the place component settled at the price reduced by the appropriate each way fraction. For example, a £5.00 each way bet on a $^{10}/_1$ winner returns £55.00 for the win part and £15.00 for the place bet given an each way fraction of $^1/_5$ of the odds. A table of each way fractions is given in figure 2.5. To calculate the place return, multiply the stake by the price and then by the fraction, before adding the original stake.

Number of Runners	Race Type	Each Way Fraction	Places
2-4		*no place betting*	
5-7	Any	$^1/_4$	1,2
8+	Non-Handicap	$^1/_5$	1,2,3
8-11	Handicap	$^1/_5$	1,2,3
12-15	Handicap	$^1/_4$	1,2,3
16+	Handicap	$^1/_4$	1,2,3,4

Figure 2.5: Table of each way fractions

Naturally, if a horse is placed but does not win, the win part of the each way bet is lost. For the previous example, had the horse been only placed the total return would have been £15.00 for an initial outlay of £10.90.

The question now arises whether it is preferable to bet to win or each way. The answer to this question is, to a certain extent, dependent on the way the selections are made. Therefore, to determine whether you should continue to place each way bets, simply calculate your profit/loss from these bets from, say, the last twelve months. Then recalculate the bets as if they had been placed to win. From the two figures you can tell immediately if you would have been better betting to win.

From a more theoretical perspective, it is possible to calculate mathematically the return rates for win only and each way betting and thus determine the best betting strategy. As an example, let us consider a five horse race with each of the runners starting at $4/1$. Putting £2.00 to win on each horse returns £10.00, the same as the total outlay (ignoring the tax component). Now what of the each way bets? Staking £1 each way on the five runners incurs the same £10.00 outlay as for the win bets. However, the return is different as given below:

From the winner: £1 at 4/1 and £1 at evens. **Return £7**
From the second: £1 at evens. **Return £2**

The total return from the each way bets is £9.00, which means that a loss has been incurred betting each way compared to a zero profit from the win bets. The loss is simply due to the each way fraction, which in the above example is $1/4$ of the odds. So, what fraction should be used to produce an equivalent (fair) return to win betting?

It is possible to calculate the fair each way fractions by considering similar examples to the one given earlier. These fractions are presented in figures 2.6 and 2.7 for non-handicap and handicap races respectively.

From figure 2.6 it can be seen that, in non-handicaps, the current fraction of $1/5$ for races of 8 or more runners represents very poor value, and as the number of runners increases the gap between the current and fair fraction widens meaning that the each way punter is receiving even poorer value.

For handicaps (figure 2.7) the picture is similar, although for races of 16 runners or more the current fraction is acceptable. Clearly, the worst case is a seven runner race when the fair fraction should be about $2/5$, nearly double the current fraction of $1/4$.

Number of Runners	Current Fraction	Fair Fraction	Places
2-4	*no place betting*		
5	0.25	0.38	1,2
6	0.25	0.40	1,2
7	0.25	0.42	1,2
8	0.20	0.24	1,2,3
9	0.20	0.25	1,2,3
10	0.20	0.26	1,2,3
12	0.20	0.27	1,2,3
14	0.20	0.28	1,2,3
16	0.20	0.29	1,2,3
20	0.20	0.30	1,2,3
25	0.20	0.31	1,2,3

Figure 2.6: Fair each way fractions for non-handicap races

Number of Runners	Current Fraction	Fair Fraction	Places
2-4	*no place betting*		
5	0.25	0.38	1,2
6	0.25	0.40	1,2
7	0.25	0.42	1,2
8	0.20	0.24	1,2,3
9	0.20	0.25	1,2,3
10	0.20	0.26	1,2,3
12	0.25	0.27	1,2,3
14	0.25	0.28	1,2,3
16	0.25	0.20	1,2,3,4
20	0.25	0.21	1,2,3,4
25	0.25	0.22	1,2,3,4

Figure 2.7: Fair each way fractions for handicap races

Therefore, each way betting seems to offer a poorer return than win only betting, except for handicaps of 16 to 20 runners where the fraction works in the bettor's favour. But perhaps the best advice is to check your own bets and determine for yourself whether the each way bets you have placed previously have shown a better profit than if the bets had been struck win only, and then use this information to structure your future betting strategy.

Multiple Bets

Of course, bettors are not restricted to win and each way singles. There is a seemingly endless array of bets the bookmakers create to tempt the cash from our wallets, however, most are based on win or each way betting.

Multiple bets are particularly popular in betting shops. A multiple bet concerns the combining of more than one horse in a single bet. For example, two selected horses can be combined in a win double. For this bet to be successful, both animals have to win, in which case the return from the first horse becomes the stake on the second. As an example, assume two horses priced at $^3/_1$ and $^4/_1$ have been combined in a £5.00 win double bet. The return would be calculated as follows:

Stake	**£5.00**	
Tax Paid:	£0.45	
Return from first horse:	£20.00	*(20 = 5 x 3 + 5)*
Return from Second Horse:	£100.00	*(100 = 20 x 4 + 20)*
Profit:	**£94.55**	

Consequently, this double pays the same as a single $^{19}/_1$ winner. In similar fashion to the each way single, an each way double also comprises two bets: a win double and a place double. Using the example given above, a £5.00 each way double on the two winners would return the following (using $^1/_4$ of the odds each way fraction):

Stake	**£10.00**	
Tax Paid:	£0.90	
Win Component (as above):	£100.00	
EW Return from first horse:	£8.75	*(8.75 = 5 x 3/4 + 5)*
Return from Second Horse:	£17.50	*(17.50 = 8.75 x 4/4 + 8.75)*
Profit	**£106.60**	*(100.00 + 17.50 - 10.90)*

The each way double has increased the profit by £12.05, however the initial £5.00 stake has been doubled to £10.00.

If the first horse had finished second and the second had won, the first part of the each way double (namely the win component) would be lost. Therefore, the return would be £17.50, a profit of £6.60. The return would be the same if both horses had been placed with neither winning. This is the advantage of the each way double. If the punter is confident that two horses will definitely be placed, providing they are both priced at an average of $^2/_1$ or more a profit will be returned if neither win but both are placed.

A variation on the each way double allows the stakes to be equally divided. Therefore, the win and place bets are not considered totally independent. For an equally divided bet the total return from the first bet is calculated and divided to form the stake for the second horse. For instance, a total return of £20.00 from the first horse would be placed at £10.00 each way on the second.

Doubles are not the only multiple bet permitted. Several selections can be combined in doubles, trebles etc. win or each way. For instance three selections comprising three singles, three doubles and a treble is a standard bet accepted by bookmakers called a *patent*. Deriving the number of combinations given several selections is a simple task using either a standard formula or by referring to a table. The formula involves *factorials*. The factorial (an exclamation mark (!) is used to denote the factorial) of a number is defined as follows:

$$n! = n \times (n-1) \times (n-2) \times \cdots \times 3 \times 2 \times 1$$

As a numerical example:

$$6! = 6 \times 5 \times 4 \times 3 \times 2 \times 1 = 720$$

The formula used to calculate the number of combinations for a specific number of items is given below, where n represents the number of selections and r represents the number of combinations. Therefore, in order to calculate the number of doubles r would have to be set to 2, and for trebles r would be set to 3 and so on.

$$\text{Number of Combinations} = \frac{n!}{r!(n-r)!}$$

Therefore, to derive the number of trebles (r=3) in 6 selections (n=6) the following equation can be used:

$$\text{Number of Trebles in 6 selections} = \frac{6!}{3! \times (6-3)!}$$

This is equivalent to $\dfrac{6 \times 5 \times 4 \times 3 \times 2 \times 1}{3 \times 2 \times 1 \times 3 \times 2 \times 1}$ which equals 20.

Consequently, picking 6 selections and betting in £5.00 trebles is equivalent to 20 separate bets in order to cover all the possible trebles. The total outlay, therefore, would be £5.00 x 20 or £100 (plus tax).

Many bookmakers display the number of combinations for different numbers of selections in table format for bettors to consult. This table is actually derived from Pascal's Triangle named after the 17th century mathematician Blaise Pascal. It is no coincidence that this eminent mathematician appears in a section on betting, since it was Pascal who, together with Pierre de Fermat, founded the theory of probability. Pascal's Triangle is easily remembered since it is organised such that each component is the sum of the two number immediately above it. The first few rows of Pascal's Triangle are given in figure 2.8.

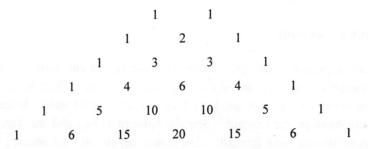

Figure 2.8: Pascal's Triangle

In order to use Pascal's Triangle to determine the number of combinations it is a simple matter of finding the correct row. In the previous example there were six selections, the correct row therefore is the sixth. This row has seven components:

	1	6	15	20	15	6	1

The first number (always a one) can be ignored and the remaining numbers represent the number of singles, doubles etc. in six selections. Consequently, there are: 6 singles, 15 doubles, 20 trebles, 15 four-folds, 6 five-folds and 1 six-fold.

The formula or Pascal's Triangle can be used to determine the number of combinations involving any number of selections. The most popular, however, seems to be four selections involving 1 four-fold, 4 trebles, and 6 doubles; this bet is known as a Yankee. Other common bets are: Super Yankee, also called a Canadian (5 selections: 10 doubles, 10 trebles, 5 four-folds and 1 five-fold), Heinz (6 selections: 15 doubles, 20 trebles, 15 four-folds, 6 five-folds, and 1 six-fold), and the Goliath (8 selections: 28 doubles, 56 trebles, 74 four-folds, 56 five-folds, 28 six-folds, 8 seven-folds, and 1 eight-fold). An important feature of these bets which should not be overlooked is the rate of increase in the number of bets as the number of selections increases. This means that the total stake placed will also rapidly increase, for a consistent unit stake.

Multiple bets offer the possibility of a large return from a relatively small outlay, and hence are quite popular. As attractive as this may seem, though, it must be remembered that these large returns are offset by the reduced chance of winning.

Forecast Betting

As an alternative to selecting the finishing position of one horse in a race, it is possible to place bets on the finishing position of two or three horses in the same event. These bets are known as forecasts. At present, bettors can choose between the Computer Straight Forecast (CSF) and the Tote Dual forecast for two horse forecasts. The former bet requires the selected horses to finish first and second in the specified order to be successful. For the Tote Dual forecast bet to succeed the named selections need only fill the first two places, the order is irrelevant.

Like all Tote bets the return from the Tote Dual forecast is determined by a pool betting system and therefore the dividend is not known until after the race has been run. Whilst the CSF is not dependent on a pool system, the return will still be unknown until after the race due to the complex nature of its calculation which is based on, amongst other things, the starting prices of all the horses in the race. However, it is possible to get a rough approximation of the likely return from the following calculation:

> add one point to the starting price of the horse selected to finish second and multiply this by the starting price of the predicted winner.

This is a pale imitation of the actual CSF calculation which, over the years, has undergone many changes to make it a more profitable bet for the bookmakers. In the excellent book *The Punter's Revenge*[2], the authors recount the *Little Owl affair* which resulted in a severe reduction of future CSF payouts involving a long priced winner. The Little Owl race featured three horses: *Little Owl* $^4/_{11}$, *Venture to Cognac* $^5/_2$ and *Great Dean* $^{66}/_1$. Clearly Little Owl was expected to win as his starting price of $^4/_{11}$ indicated. However, the favourite was pulled up in the race leaving Venture to Cognac to beat Great Dean. The CSF paid the equivalent to $^{141}/_1$. However, after this result the formula for calculating the CSF was amended with the introduction of the *harmonic factor* which *accounted* for long priced horses in small fields. As a result of this modification the equivalent CSF for this race based on the new formula would produce a payout of just $^{14}/_1$. This, and subsequent, modifications to the formula have made the CSF a bet to avoid, since in the long term it is almost impossible for bettors to return a profit from the CSF.

There are two bets which allow for the forecast of the first three horses in a race: the tricast and Tote Trifecta. These bets are directly comparable to the CSF and Dual Forecast previously mentioned. Both require the bettor to correctly predict the first three horses in finishing order, with the dividend from the tricast determined by a formula and for the Trifecta from the total pool bet on the race. Like the CSF the formula for calculating the tricast dividend has undergone many changes, not least the 1996 modification which reduces the payout for horses which are involved in the finish and started from consecutive stalls (see *Effect of the Draw* section). Like the CSF the tricast now offers very poor value and bettors are recommended to opt for the Tote Trifecta.

When to Bet with the Tote

The merits of the Tote compared to bookmakers' returns have already been discussed with respect to forecast betting. This theme continues in this section with attention focused on win and place betting.

A comparison between the Tote win return and the returned starting price for the winners of over 660 randomly selected races run in 1996 is given in figures 2.9 and 2.10.

Number of Runners	Average S.P. Return[†]	Comparable Tote Return[†]
2-4	2.77	1.89
5-7	3.89	3.68
8-12	5.17	5.56
13+	9.10	11.50
All	**5.91**	**6.68**

[†] *Excluding stake*

Figure 2.9: Tote return against average S.P.
return by number of runners

Figure 2.9 compares the returns by the number of runners in each race. It can be seen that in small fields the starting price offers a better return, however as the size of field increases the Tote return is generally higher. And for all races the Tote return is approximately 0.8 of a point higher than the starting price. This is equivalent to getting a free $^4/_5$ winner with every successful bet placed on the Tote. In figure 2.10 a similar analysis is presented, with starting price replacing the number of runners.

Figure 2.10 also provides strong evidence for supporting the Tote, except this analysis shows that the improved Tote returns are found when the starting price exceeds $^5/_1$. The longer priced horses tend to be under-bet by punters and consequently return a higher dividend on the Tote. However this lack of interest does not apparently result in inflated starting prices with the bookmakers.

This is important information for punters who are unable to take an early price or early show about their selections. When betting at starting price, and the selection is likely to start longer than $^5/_1$, it would seem sensible to bet on the Tote.

Starting Price	Average S.P. Return[†]	Comparable Tote Return[†]
Odds On	0.60	0.62
Evens - 2/1	1.52	1.45
85/40 - 5/1	3.59	3.51
11/2 - 10/1	7.55	8.10
11/1 - 16/1	13.30	15.41
18/1+	25.00	36.52
All	**5.91**	**6.68**

[†] *Excluding stake*

Figure 2.10: Tote return against average S.P.
return by starting price

Analyses for the place returns for the same 660 races are given in figures 2.11 and 2.12. Again, a similar pattern emerges for the analysis by number of runners (figure 2.11) with the Tote return performing best in relation to the starting price return for races with larger fields (i.e. 13 or more runners).

Number of Runners	Average Place Return[†] at S.P.	Average Tote Place Return[†]
5-7	1.23	1.22
8-12	1.53	1.44
13+	2.19	2.55
All	**1.75**	**1.80**

[†] *Excluding stake*

Figure 2.11: Tote place return against average
S.P. place return by number of runners

The analysis by starting price (figure 2.12) shows that the Tote return is nearly equal, or higher, than the starting price return for all categories. However, in similar fashion to the win analysis, the Tote place return is clearly better for the longer priced horses. This is due to the general level of under-pricing associated with these runners and the poor each way fractions currently used by bookmakers.

Starting Price	Average Place Return[†] at S.P.	Average Tote Place Return[†]
Odds On	0.14	0.20
Evens - 2/1	0.34	0.37
85/40 - 5/1	0.77	0.80
11/2 - 10/1	1.57	1.53
11/1 - 16/1	2.74	2.95
18/1+	5.70	6.20
All	**1.75**	**1.80**

[†] *Excluding stake*

Figure 2.12: Tote place return against average
S.P. place return by starting price

Spread Betting

Though still in its infancy, spread betting has become a very popular means of betting in the last few years. Unlike normal betting where a winner is simply treated as a winner regardless of the winning margin, with spread betting it is the manner of the victory, or defeat, which is of importance. The spread betting options for the outcome of a football match, for instance, would include the superiority of one team over their opponents in terms of goals. A spread would be set, for example team A over team B at 0.9 - 1.2 goals. *Buying* the goal difference at 1.2 would mean that the team would need to win by more than 1.2 goals for the bet to be successful. A win by two clear goals would return a profit of 0.8 multiplied by the stake. It is also possible to *sell* at 0.9, hoping for the team to win by less than 0.9 goals, in other words to draw or lose. Spread betting is closely linked to the commodities market where the speculators gamble on the future price of a commodity. If the contract is bought and the price of the commodity increases, the speculator is able to close at the new price and make a profit. However, if the price declines, closing the contract would result in a loss. For horseracing spread bets are offered on pairs of horses racing against each other (i.e. a spread on the distance one horse may finish in front of another), or the total winning distances for a day's racing, amongst many other options.

The main problem with spread betting is that the likely return is unknown when the bet is placed since it is dependent on the final superiority measure. The total loss which may be incurred is also unknown and consequently in extreme circumstances the loss could be substantial even for a small unit stake. However, the spreads are generally updated during the event, therefore, to reduce the impact of a very poor result it is possible to place another, opposing, bet to minimise losses. Spread betting is for experienced bettors and, before opening an spread account the pros and cons of this form of betting need to be considered very carefully.

References

[1] *Raceform, The Official Formbook*, published by Raceform, Newbury, Berks.
[2] *The Punter's Revenge - Computers in the world of gambling*, by Tony Drapkin and Richard Forsyth, Chapman and Hall/Methuen, London, 1987.

3

Race Analysis

Chapter 2 provided a summary of general information relating to horseracing in Great Britain. In this chapter attention is turned to the more specific task of analysing horses and races. Before developing a forecasting model for horseracing, the raw data needs to be pre-processed and transformed into a format usable by the model. Several methods are proposed in the following sections which can be used to evaluate many critical factors, or features, that constitute the profile of a horse. These profiles then form part of the input to the forecasting model. However, before this detailed examination of race data, the predictability of horseraces in general is considered.

The Predictability of Horseraces

So, predicting the results of horseraces is a complex but tractable problem. Or is it? In this section the predictability of horseraces is examined and it is discussed whether the outcome of a race is purely the result of random processes or can be determined prior to the event.

The sequence of numbers produced by recording the outcomes of many rolls of a fair dice is random. Similarly, the spin of a roulette wheel and the numbers selected for the National Lottery (or 49's draw). All three events produce sequences of numbers for which no apparent pattern exists and therefore can be considered to be random. Since the aim of prediction is to determine rules and laws which can explain an event, or organise the observations into some meaningful pattern, there seems little point trying to predict the outcome of these random events which, by definition, are unpredictable. If the results of horseraces exhibited the same degree of randomness there would be no point in pursuing appropriate forecasting solutions. Fortunately horseracing is not entirely random which can be illustrated quite simply by comparing the winners to runners success rate for an observable factor relating to each horse, namely the starting price.

Figure 3.1 presents the number of winners, runners, and success ratio for over 200,000 race performances by starting price.

Starting Price	Number of Winners	Number of Runners	% Strike Rate
Odds On	1610	2718	59.2%
Evens-2/1	3104	8353	37.2%
85/40-5/1	6259	32081	19.5%
11/2-10/1	4928	50587	9.7%
11/1-20/1	2330	57162	4.1%
22/1-40/1	408	31452	1.3%
50/1+	53	13756	0.4%

Figure 3.1: Analysis by starting price

If the results of horseraces were entirely random the percentage column would simply reflect the proportion of horses which started within each price band. In fact there is a clearly observable pattern to the proportions of winners with the strike rate decreasing as the starting price increases. The starting price for each horse is based on the final prices available at the racecourse which are in turn formed by the on-course bookmakers and then modified by the weight of betting money, and hence form a prediction of the outcome of the race. If races were entirely random this measure, or prediction, would not be reflected in the winner to runners success ratio. Consequently, we must conclude that the results of horseraces are not due to purely random forces but are, in fact, predictable.

Although the results of horseraces are not completely random, a high degree of uncertainty still exists. It is this uncertainty which makes the horseracing problem worthy of study. In many games of chance, such as roulette, dice and the National Lottery, the uncertainty does not exist. Whilst the outcome of any one spin of the roulette wheel, roll of the dice, or drop of the lottery ball is unknown before the event (i.e. it is a random event), the *probability* of each outcome can be computed exactly. For example, with an unbiased dice, the probability of a two being thrown on the next roll is $^1/_6$. This probability is mathematically defined and proven, and hence no uncertainty exists. Consequently, it is a straightforward task to establish fair odds for these events. In the dice rolling case the fair odds for throwing a two would be $^5/_1$. In this case, though, neither bettor nor bookmaker would return a long term profit since the odds equate to the probability. With horseracing the probability of any horse winning a race remains inexact and hence will result in differences in opinion between bettor and bookmaker, making betting a viable proposition, in some cases.

Evaluating Horseraces

In Chapter 1 the importance of data pre-processing was discussed and several techniques were proposed including feature extraction and the use of prior knowledge. From the available literature (for instance, Flat Racing for Profit[1], Horse Race Selection and Betting[2], and Betting for a Living[3]), it was found that seven key elements, or features, of an animal's profile are most often used in any evaluation of its potential race success. These elements are: ability, age, weight carried (for handicap races), suitability of race conditions, assessment of recent performances, likely level of fitness, and previous success rate. In addition two other components, namely the ability of the jockey and trainer, are also used for classification methods. Consequently, nine components form the profile of each horse.

Sources of Information

The evaluation of these nine critical factors depends on historical information. For example, to determine whether a horse is suited by the prevailing ground conditions requires an examination of the animal's previous race performances on a similar surface. The main source of this information is the daily and weekly racing press, specifically the *Racing Post*, *Weekender* and *Raceform Update*. These papers contain details of the day's racecards including lists of runners, owners, trainers, the weight each horse is set to carry, declared jockeys and a betting forecast. In addition, horse specific information is also included such as ratings (see *Assessment of Ability* section), and details of previous race performances together with race analyses written by expert tipsters.

To get an even more thorough analysis of previous races (trade papers generally only give details of the three most recent runs for each horse) it is possible to subscribe to a formbook in either paper or computerised form, for instance Raceform, the Official Formbook. The formbook provides details of every race run in Great Britain, as well as some foreign races. Details of every runner in the race plus the distance beaten, betting details and race time are supplemented by a brief comment on each performance. Whilst the formbook provides the raw data on a race-by-race basis with which to work, other publications, such as the Timeform Black Book, give summaries in a horse-by-horse format. These summaries basically provide conclusions which the Timeform race analysts derive from the race data. Consequently, the details are presented in a readable format and include references to the likely preferences of each horse and an assessment of its ability in the form of a rating.

In recent years racing data has also been available on the Internet (for a subscription fee), for instance an overnight service is offered by Raceform. And computerised formbooks, which are updated on a weekly basis (or more frequently if required), provide detailed information plus the raw data for building forecasting models. Whether you choose to use the daily press, a formbook or the Internet, you will find that racing form is expensive but essential.

Evaluating the Key Components

In this section methods for evaluating the critical factors which make-up a animal's profile are considered. These features will then form the input data for each of the forecasting models discussed in Chapters 5-7. It has been assumed that the race analyst has access to a formbook and/or the daily racing press in the formulation of these techniques.

Assessment of Ability

Ability ratings form the cornerstone of many forecasting methods. The aim of these ratings is to *quantify* the ability of each horse and express this ability on a standard scale. This transformation allows several horses to be compared and ranked with respect to their perceived ability. Two main categories of ability ratings exist: form ratings and speed ratings. An example of a form rating is the handicap rating discussed earlier. Form ratings are deduced by handicappers and are based on the finishing position of one horse relative to another. When assessing a race, often handicappers will look for a horse which they believe runs consistently and adjust the ratings of the other runners relative to this horse. Form ratings are expressed in pounds using variations on the conversion table given in figure 2.1 (Chapter 2). Many racing organisations provide (for a price) their own form ratings, though ratings are also published daily in the Racing Post. As an example consider figure 3.2 which shows the ability ratings published by Raceform for the 1997 Champion Stakes, a Group 1 non-juvenile race run at Newmarket in October.

RHR	Horse *(Age-Weight)*	Last No	Last Three Ratings		
152	Pilsudski *(5-9-2)*	4665a	147	152	146
142	Benny The Dip *(3-8-11)*	3646	145	145	136
138	Revoque *(3-8-11)*	4422	125	138	116
136	Bahhare *(3-8-11)*	4422	136	136	136
135+	Stowaway *(3-8-11)*	3647	135	134	123
135	Loup Sauvage *(3-8-11)*	4392a	129	135	132
135	Bijou d'Inde *(3-8-11)*	4356	103	98	74

Figure 3.2: Example of form ratings

Although four form ratings are given per horse, the most important is in the leftmost column, before the name of the runner. The remaining three ratings simply indicate the animal's most recent race performances. In this example Pilsudski was given the highest form rating (152) ten pounds superior to the second highest rated horse, Benny The Dip, at 142. A ten pounds difference, as in this example, is quite significant which was reflected in Pilsudski's starting price of evens. In the race Pilsudski won by two lengths (equivalent to 3lbs) from Loup Sauvage who could have been considered to have run better than expected and would probably be rated higher for his next run as a result.

Speed ratings, also referred to as *time figures*, do not rely on form but instead are based on race times. The speed figure calculation can become very complex depending on the number of factors the system designer decides to include. Simply comparing race times is of little use due to the differences in racecourse configuration and variability of going. When calculating speed figures it is necessary to account for these variations or the resultant figures will be extremely misleading. Using a *standard* race time for each race track solves the problem of course configuration. Standard times represent the time a horse rated 100 by the BHB is likely to take to run a particular course on good to firm going. Incorporating standard times facilitates the comparison of horses running at different tracks, but does not account for varying states of going. To quantify the going effect it is necessary to calculate a *course going allowance* for each day's racing. This allowance is derived from the differences between the race times and the standard times, and once calculated can be used to generate comparable speed figures. However, rather than performing this calculation every day it is possible to purchase speed figures from most racing organisations. Speed figures are also published in the daily, and weekly, trade press.

There are many ways to represent ratings in a forecasting model. A common approach is to standardise the ratings to the highest rated horse in each race. In other words, each rating is subtracted from the highest rating in the race with this difference used in the model. Naturally, using this method the highest rated horse will have a standardised rating of zero. Using this standardised form it is possible to determine the importance (accuracy) of the ratings. Figure 3.3 presents an analysis of Raceform's Private handicap ratings for over 400 randomly selected races.

Adjusted	Juveniles			Non-Juveniles		
Rating	Wins	Runs	%	Wins	Runs	%
0	42	169	24.9	81	458	17.7
1..5	29	184	15.8	137	1079	12.7
6..10	27	224	12.1	107	1045	10.2
11..15	22	196	11.2	39	557	7.0
16..20	7	132	5.3	15	262	5.7
21..30	7	149	4.7	13	243	5.3
31..50	1	101	1.0	5	158	3.2
51+	0	41	0.0	0	33	0.0
All	135	1196	11.3	397	3835	10.4

Figure 3.3: Analysis of standardised form ratings

Clearly, the form ratings analysed in figure 3.3 are of predictive value with the success ratio for top-rated horses significantly exceeding the average rate, although this is slightly misleading when considering the overall trend. By definition of the standardising procedure, all races include a horse rated zero, however, the rating of the second best horse differs greatly from race to race. In some cases, the top rated horse will have, as its nearest rival, a horse rated, say, 10, and consequently, a good winning opportunity. In contrast, every horse rated 1 will always have an animal rated zero to overcome, and thus theoretically face a more difficult task. Therefore, analysing the ratings in isolation does not accurately reflect the relative differences between them. Intuitively, the success ratio should follow a linear trend, but since there is always a horse rated zero, and not necessarily any horses rated close to zero, the winners to runners success ratio for top rated horses is over stated compared to the other ratings. However, there are several techniques which can be used to overcome this minor difficulty when modelling the data which are discussed in later chapters. Assessing the ability of the runners is a critical part of race analysis with ability ratings forming the basis of most forecasting models.

Age

The better flat racehorses tend to stop racing after their three- or four-year-old seasons much to the disappointment of their supporters. This policy is hardly surprising, and difficult to criticise, given the relatively low levels of prize-money in this country compared to the potentially high stud values. Racing a top class colt beyond its three-year-old season is a risky proposition. The potential gain of prize-money from three, maybe four races is insignificant compared to the stud fees alone. However, the main risk is in respect to injury or poor racing performance. Although rare, it is possible that the animal could sustain a fatal injury whilst training or racing. The risk of poor race performance is greater though. The horse may not *train on* from three to four years old and perform well below expectations as a four-year-old. This would have a significant effect on its potential stud value and hence reduce the total financial return to the owner. Some animals, however, are campaigned for many seasons with a few still racing after they have reached double figures in age. The age of a horse is often overlooked by the bettor when making a selection, but as figure 3.4 shows it is a factor that should be considered.

Age of Horse	Number of Winners	Number of Runners	% Strike Rate
3	4883	49861	9.8
4	2100	23934	8.8
5	1278	12634	10.1
6	677	7465	9.1
7	370	4433	8.3
8	187	2382	7.9
9+	166	2274	7.3
All	**9661**	**102983**	**9.4**

Figure 3.4: Analysis by age

From figure 3.4 it can be seen that the younger horses have a better wins to runs success rate, with seemingly a significant decrease in the percentage from ages six to seven years. A further drop in the strike rate occurs when the age of the horse exceeds eight years. Consequently, when considering all-age races it would seem appropriate to account for the ages of the runners in the model.

Weight Carried

Although the age of a horse appears to have a slight bearing on its probability of success, the amount of weight carried by horses in handicap races is a much stronger indicator. It is important to remember that the aim of artificial handicapping is to give each horse an equal chance of winning, and therefore in handicap races the wins to runs ratio for horses in different weight bands should be uniform. However, this is not the case. Consider figure 3.5 which shows the strike rate for horses running in juvenile handicaps by weight carried.

From figure 3.5 a strong correlation can be seen between the amount of weight carried and the probability of success. However, the correlation is positive with the chance of winning increasing with the amount of weight carried. This is in direct contrast to the aim of handicapping which is to reduce the superiority of the better horses by increasing the weight they carry in the race. From figure 3.6 it can be seen that a similar pattern is generated by non-juvenile handicappers. Additionally, this pattern is also found

Weight Carried (st-lbs)	Number of Winners	Number of Runners	% Strike Rate
9-08 - 10-00	3	17	17.6
9-01 - 9-07	139	1014	13.7
8-08 - 9-00	107	1133	9.4
8-01 - 8-07	65	990	6.6
7-08 - 8-00	22	503	4.4
7-00 - 7-07	10	338	3.0
All	346	3995	8.7

Figure 3.5: Analysis by weight band for nurseries

Weight Carried (st-lbs)	Number of Winners	Number of Runners	% Strike Rate
9-08 - 10-00	789	6979	11.3
9-01 - 9-07	1257	12617	10.0
8-08 - 9-00	1044	12881	8.1
8-01 - 8-07	723	9916	7.3
7-08 - 8-00	270	4652	5.8
7-00 - 7-07	132	3241	4.1
All	4215	50286	8.4

Figure 3.6: Analysis by weight band for non-juvenile handicaps

in Jump racing as reported in *Jump Racing For Profit*[4].

Figures 3.5 and 3.6 seem to imply that giving a horse more weight increases its chance of winning. This is clearly absurd since the more weight a horse has to carry the slower it will run, and hence the likelihood of success is diminished. So, how can the results presented in the above tables be explained? Firstly, it should be remembered that the best horse in the race carries most weight. Horses at the top of the handicap have shown the best public form, and within the bounds of a race the horses set to carry the most weight have performed to a higher standard than those weighted below them. Secondly, for a horse to occupy a high position in the handicap it needs to produce a high level of form over several races. In other words, these horses are probably more consistent and likely to reproduce previous race form. Finally, the better horses judged on ability also possess other valuable qualities such as a strong desire to win. It is far preferably to support a horse which is likely to give its true running and try its best to win over an equally matched horse (in terms of form or speed) which may have a doubtful temperament.

Based on the above data the amount of weight carried appears to be a very important factor when assessing handicap races, and should not be over-looked when building forecasting models.

Recent Race Performances

So far the evaluation of these critical components has been simply a matter of analysing the factor (i.e. weight carried or age) by the number of winners and losers. However, when evaluating a race performance there is no explicit measure of good or poor performance for each horse as in the case of age, for instance, where each horse is attributed an age on a discrete scale from 2 to 15. Consequently, it is necessary to determine a set of rules which can be used to classify a race performance. An analysis of this measure by winners and losers will then indicate its importance.

There are several different methods, and several different variables, that can be used to evaluate race performances. For example, finishing position, in absolute terms or expressed as a percentage of the number of runners in the race, can be combined with a threshold value to form a classification scheme. For example, in rule form:

> if   position of horse is first or second
> then race performance is good

Alternatively, finishing position can be replaced by distance beaten and a different threshold value chosen, such as 4 lengths. On a slightly more sophisticated level, individual race ratings can be used. A rating can be generated for each race in which a horse runs and can be compared to the animal's best rating to determine the level of performance. As an example:

> if   today's rating > 90% of expected rating
> then horse has run well

These methods, though, are not independent of the other factors influencing the race result. The horse may be ridden by a very inexperienced jockey, for instance, or the trainer may be undergoing a lean spell with regard to winners, or the horse may not be suited by the configuration of the track. All these reasons may affect the running of a horse which is *in form* and running to the best of its ability given the circumstances.

One variable which does account for these additional factors is the starting price. Since the starting price is a consensus of opinion between bettors and bookmakers taking into account all available information it is a good guide to the likelihood of success. This was shown in figure 3.1 where the winners to runners strike rate declined as the starting price increased. Consequently, the starting price can be used as a forecast of the *expected* finishing position of a horse given all the relevant factors, and hence can identify good and poor race performances. Figure 3.7 shows the cumulative percentage of runners by distance beaten and starting price. In order to make this table applicable to all race distances, the distance beaten is given in pounds using the conversion method highlighted in Chapter 2 (figure 2.1).

Distance Beaten (pounds)	Starting Price						
	Odds On	Evens - 2/1	85/40 - 5/1	11/2 - 10/1	11/1 - 20/1	22/1 - 40/1	50/1+
0	56.9%	37.3%	19.3%	9.8%	4.3%	1.5%	0.4%
0-0.1	64.7%	46.2%	27.3%	15.0%	7.0%	2.7%	0.8%
0-2.0	69.5%	53.0%	34.0%	20.0%	10.0%	4.0%	1.3%
0-4.0	78.6%	65.1%	46.6%	30.9%	17.5%	7.8%	2.6%
0-8.0	84.2%	73.8%	56.5%	41.0%	25.5%	13.1%	4.8%
0-12.0	89.5%	81.3%	67.7%	53.0%	37.0%	21.5%	9.7%
0-18.0	94.9%	89.3%	80.4%	69.6%	55.8%	38.7%	21.6%
0-30.0	97.7%	94.6%	89.9%	83.9%	74.7%	60.6%	42.4%
0-50.0	98.9%	97.0%	94.8%	91.4%	85.9%	76.3%	62.0%
All	100.0%	100.0%	100.0%	100.0%	100.0%	100.0%	100.0%

Figure 3.7: Analysis of distance beaten by starting price

From figure 3.7 it can be seen that over half (56.9%) of horses starting at odds on are successful with only 0.4% of horses priced at $^{50}/_1$ or more winning. This further validates the hypothesis that the starting price provides an accurate guide to the likely distance beaten.

Although figure 3.7 provides the basis for determining a classification scheme for discriminating between race performances a third component, namely the threshold value (in this case a percentage), needs to be chosen by the race analyst. The choice of threshold is somewhat arbitrary, however its selection will have a significant effect on the classifications. For instance, selecting the threshold at 75% would mean that horses starting at $^{11}/_1$ or more would be classified as producing a good race performance if beaten up to the equivalent of 30lbs (10 lengths in a 5 furlong sprint or 24 lengths in a 1½ mile race). A 75% threshold would also mean that 75% of all race performances would be categorised as *good*.

A threshold that has been found to work well is the median value (i.e. 50%). Using this value the following rules identify *good* race performances:

> *if   starting price is odds-on*
> *and   distance beaten <= 0 lbs*
> *then performance is good*

> *if   starting price greater than $^{49}/_1$*
> *and   distance beaten <= 40 lbs*
> *then performance is good*

Clearly, to implement this approach one rule is required for each price band. Alternatively these rules can be replaced by a single equation which adequately approximates the system:

> *if   distance beaten (lbs) <= starting price*
> *then performance is good*

Although this single rule works well it does allow high priced horses to be beaten by considerable distances and still be classified as running well. For instance, a horse beaten the equivalent of 50lbs could be classified as running well simply because its starting price indicated that it had little chance of winning. To prevent this from happening it is possible to introduce an additional threshold which all horses must satisfy regardless of starting price. For example, all horses must finish within a distance equivalent to 10lbs of the winner. Modifying the above rule produces the following:

> *if   distance beaten (lbs) <= starting price*
> *and distance beaten <= 10 lbs*
> *then performance is good*

Using a similar approach, rules can be generated for classifying *poor* race performances. A threshold of 80% converts to the following equation-based rule:

> *if   distance beaten (lbs) >= 3* x *starting price + 8*
> *then race performance is poor*

This rule would classify a horse starting at odds on as running poorly if beaten more than the equivalent of 11lbs, or $3^2/_3$ lengths in a 5 furlong race or almost nine lengths in a 1½ mile race.

Now that a classification scheme for race performances has been identified, it is possible to test the significance of recent race performances, and whether recent form can be used to predict future success. Figure 3.8 details the success rate of horses based on their previous race performance. It can be seen that horses which were classified as running poorly (using the above rules) in their most recent race have a strike rate in their next race of only 4.3%, this compares to 13.6% for horses classified as running well in their latest race. A race performance of neither good nor poor is labelled moderate, and horses in this group score at a rate of 8.9% on their next run. This is encouraging evidence and clearly indicates the importance of recent form.

Figures 3.9 and 3.10 show the same analysis for the second most recent, and third most recent run. A similar trend to that highlighted in figure 3.8 is apparent although, as would be expected, the differences between the percentages is not as great.

Race Performance	Number of Winners	Number of Runners	% Strike Rate
Poor	3	69	4.3%
Moderate	39	437	8.9%
Good	32	236	13.6%
All	74	742	10.0%

Figure 3.8: Analysis of most recent race

Race Performance	Number of Winners	Number of Runners	% Strike Rate
Poor	5	59	8.5%
Moderate	35	406	8.6%
Good	23	206	11.2%
All	63	671	9.4%

Figure 3.9: Analysis of second most recent race

Race Performance	Number of Winners	Number of Runners	% Strike Rate
Poor	5	67	7.5%
Moderate	30	370	8.1%
Good	23	175	13.1%
All	58	612	9.5%

Figure 3.10: Analysis of third most recent race

The rules given in this section for evaluating race performances are in a very simple format and are based on only two variables. Naturally, the real world situation is very different and many other factors could be considered. For example, the finishing distances between horses tends to increase as the ground softens, therefore the inclusion of a going variable in the rules may result in more accurate assessments. Furthermore, the rules do not account for other exceptions, such as horses running poorly due to lameness. Analysis of the race comment which is attached to every performance could highlight these circumstances. Special cases which can be determined from the race comment include: finished lame, eased by jockey, fell, unseated jockey, hampered near finish. A simple examination of the race comment could reclassify some horses which may have appeared to run poorly into an additional *unknown* category.

Suitability of Race Conditions

It is possible to use the method developed for assessing race performances to establish the suitability of specific race conditions. In this section rules are created which can be used to determine the suitability of the going and race distance for any horse. The section concludes with an examination of the effect of the draw, which on some courses, is of paramount importance.

Suitability of Ground Conditions

The state of the going plays a significant role in the outcome of every horse race run on the turf in Great Britain. Ground conditions can vary from *hard* (the driest ground) to *heavy* (the softest ground) depending on the recent weather pattern and the use of irrigation facilities on the track. Although there are seven classifications of going (see Chapter 2), it is the extremes of going which have greatest effect on the race results.

Horses tend to be suited by either firm (fast) or soft surfaces, although a few animals will perform equally well on all types of going. The type of going a horse prefers is often determined by its physique and running style. For instance, horses which display a high knee action are often found to be suited by softer surfaces, and in many cases the going preferences of the sire will be passed to his offspring. However, in order to determine the suitability of a particular state of ground the most informative data are the past race performances by the horse. All the racing experts interviewed prior to developing these techniques agree that horses which have run well on a particular surface can be assumed to be suited by it. Therefore, using the race performance rule from the previous section, rules of the following type can be developed:

> *if   today's going is good*
> *and the horse has performed well on good going*
> *then today's going is suitable*

Although this type of rule is very simplistic it seems to perform well. Figure 3.11 presents an analysis of this measure for 85 randomly selected races. Clearly, horses with proven form on the prevailing going have a better chance of success.

Going Suitability Conclusion	Number of Winners	Number of Runners	% Strike Rate
proven form on prevailing going	50	378	13.2%
no proven form on prevailing going	35	495	7.1%
All	**85**	**873**	**9.7%**

Figure 3.11: Suitability of the going

Suitability of Race Distance

If there is one thing which can be guaranteed to happen in racing every year it is the debate concerning the likelihood of the Derby favourite staying the 1½ mile distance at Epsom. This debate generally starts in early May, after the first two classics have been run, and continues to Derby day itself in June, and sometimes even beyond. This debate is even more intense if the Derby favourite happens to be the 2,000 Guineas winner. Pedigree experts are asked to comment on the animal's optimum race distance based on the race performances of its sire, dam, grandsire, etc., whilst form experts ponder over the horse's running style. The jockey, trainer, owner and stable lad are all queried on the matter, but the fact remains that until the race no-one knows for sure whether the horse will appreciate the distance or not.

As with human athletes, thoroughbred horses are suited by specific race distances which can be broadly categorised into sprinting, middle distance and staying races. For a horse to perform to its best ability it needs to be racing over the correct distance, and therefore the suitability of the race distance is considered to be of critical importance by most race analysts.

Although a similar process can be followed to that used in evaluating the suitability of the going, an additional time factor needs to be considered for race distances. Apart from the specialist sprinters, thoroughbreds tend to appreciate longer race distances as they mature. For illustration, currently, the longest race contested by juveniles is 10 furlongs, whereas for older horses this would only be considered to be a middle distance race.

The time modification takes the form of including, in the evaluation, only those previous races which satisfy the specific criterion given in figure 3.12.

Age of Horse	Historical races included
two-year-old horses	all races
three-year-old horses	all races within the last 365 days
older horses (4yo+)	all races except juvenile runs

Figure 3.12: Time restriction for suitability of race distance assessment

One other difference from the going assessment procedure is that while going is expressed in discrete form (i.e. there are seven separate categories), race distances are continuous. This slightly complicates the comparison between the race under consideration and historical races. A simple solution, and the one adopted here, is to use ranges of race distances and to consider two races to be matched with respect to distance if they differ by up to ½ furlong. Consequently, the rules take the following form:

> *if   today's going is 10 furlongs*
> *and   the horse has performed well at 10 furlongs ± ½f*
> *and   time criterion satisfied*
> *then today's race distance is suitable*

To determine the importance of the suitability of race distance 557 horses were analysed, the results of which are given in figure 3.13. Clearly, this is an important variable since from figure 3.13 it can be seen that horses with proven form over the race distance have a success ratio of almost twice that of horses without proven form over the race distance.

Race Distance Suitability Conclusion	Number of Winners	Number of Runners	% Strike Rate
proven form over this distance ± ½f	43	398	10.8%
no proven form over this distance ± ½f	9	159	5.7%
All	**52**	**557**	**9.3%**

Figure 3.13: Suitability of race distance

The Effect of the Draw

The size and shape of Britain's racecourses varies enormously, from the small almost circular Chester to the figure of eight course at Windsor. One attribute that all courses share though is the use of starting stalls. These were introduced in Great Britain in the 1960's after continued pressure from the founder of the Timeform organisation, Phil Bull.

The aim of starting stalls is to produce an even break for all the runners, which is especially important in sprint races. The allocation of stall numbers to the runners at the overnight stage determines their starting stall positions, and to a certain extent the part of the track over which they will run: near side, far side or centre. Obviously, the ultimate position of the horse relative to the other runners and the running rail is determined by the jockey, however the stall number (or *draw*) plays an important part in the positioning of the runners. And this can have a marked effect on the eventual race result.

There are several ways in which the draw can affect the outcome of a race. Firstly, moisture is not necessarily retained uniformly across the width of the course, consequently the horses running on the softer, or slower, side will be at a considerable disadvantage. Naturally, non-uniform moisture retention is especially apparent on cambered tracks with the lower part of the course retaining water for a longer period of time. Such variability in the ground conditions becomes more significant in sprint races where horses tend not to group together. Over longer distances the runners tend to bunch together soon after the start thus minimising the effect of the softer ground. Secondly, horses often run better when positioned close to a running rail. The rail prevents the horse from wandering across the track (at least in one direction) keeping its path to the line straighter. And thirdly, on round courses, horses drawn on the inside will benefit from taking the shortest route from starting stall to finishing line. All of the these factors can influence the outcome of a race.

The effect of the draw is published in most racing publications (daily papers, formbooks etc.), however, whilst these assessments indicate whether high or low numbers are preferred, they do not attempt to quantify the effect. Consequently, it is difficult to incorporate this information into forecasting models. For example, if for a particular course high numbers are considered to hold the advantage, would a horse starting from stall 15 in a race with 20 runners be classified as well drawn? Furthermore, how much is the horse in stall 20 favoured over the horse in stall 10? To answer these questions, and provide information which can be included into forecasting procedures, it is necessary to know by how much one stall is favoured over another in terms of distance (i.e. 2 lengths better).

In order to quantify the draw effect it is necessary to analyse a sample of races for every race distance at each track. The population from which this sample is selected for analysis in this section constitutes all non-juvenile handicap races run during the four seasons from 1993-1997. Handicap races are chosen in preference to non-handicaps since the ability range of the runners is normalised by the allocation of different weights by the BHB handicappers, therefore only a small external effect will make a noticeable change to the result of the race. In non-handicaps the ability range is likely to be much wider, and even with the best draw of the race and a ten lengths start a large proportion of the runners would still fail to win. In other words, the draw will not, in most cases, be a significant determining factor in non-handicaps, the crucial element being the ability of the horses. A similar argument can be applied to nurseries, although not to quite the same extent. Unexposed two-year-old horses are exceptionally difficult to handicap and therefore the differing abilities will not be accounted for as well as they are for older horses.

Whilst an analysis of the success rates of horses running from each stall will indicate whether high or low numbers are favoured on a particular track, this will not provide an explicit numerical value of the advantage afforded to each runner. In order to determine the effect in terms of distance advantage it is necessary to consider the distance between the horses at the finish by stall number. However, simply analysing the average distance each horse is beaten by the race winner on a stall-by-stall basis would yield biased results. Since the allocation of stall numbers always starts from one, in small fields the winner must be drawn low; and in large fields for the horses drawn high to win they must overcome more opponents. It is possible to remove this bias, though, by considering the distance each horse is beaten by the runner drawn in a specific stall, say stall one. On this basis the average distance beaten for all horses in stall one will be zero. For the other stalls, a positive average distance beaten indicates that these stalls are disadvantaged by the draw compared to stall one. A negative value indicates a draw advantage compared to stall one. In figure 3.14 this analysis is presented in graphical form for the 5 furlong course at Chester.

From figure 3.14 it can be seen that, on average, the horses drawn high are at a disadvantage compared to the stall one runner. For instance, the horses in stall 16 beaten, on average, by about 6 lengths by the horses running from stall one for the races analysed. This is not surprising since Chester is a tight, circular left-handed course, and consequently the horses drawn wide have further to race than those drawn on the inside. Fitting a trend line to these data indicates that the disadvantage to horses drawn in stalls other than stall one is equivalent to 0.45 lengths per stall. In other words a horse drawn in stall 5 has a disadvantage of approximately 2¼ lengths (i.e. 0.45x5) to overcome which equates to 6¾lbs using the distance to weight conversion given in Chapter 2.

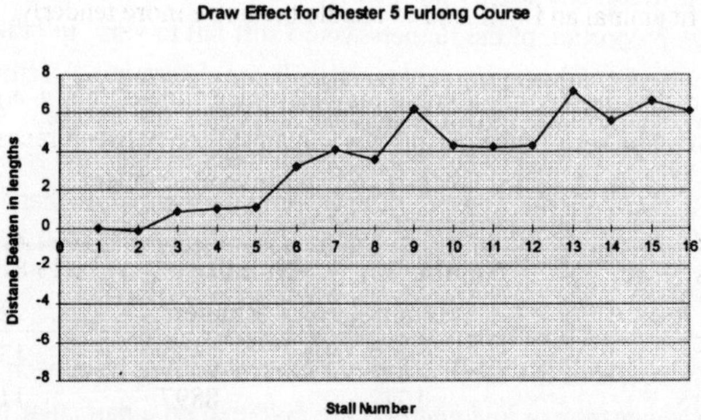

Draw Effect for Chester 5 Furlong Course

Figure 3.14: Analysis of the draw effect

On some tracks the positioning of the starting stalls and the state of the going can also effect the draw. However, this is easily accounted for in the analysis by isolating particular track conditions and considering each set separately. For instance analysing races run on soft or heavy ground separately from fast ground events.

The average winning distance in 5 furlong handicap races (i.e. between the winner and the second) is a little over 1 length, so a draw effect similar to the one at Chester is clearly significant. Once quantified this factor can either be included in the model as a separate variable or used to adjust the ability ratings of the runners. This factor is of such significance though, that it can be used without considering any other data to form a successful prediction model, and this is discussed further in Chapter 5.

Fitness

Not all horses are 100% fit to race when they reach the starting stalls. In the trade press trainers will often be quoted as saying their horse will "need the run" before it returns to the course after a break, and jockeys regularly report that particular horses will "improve for the run" after an introductory race. Many people find this hard to believe; why would a trainer enter an unfit horse? Apparently, it is extremely difficult to get a horse to complete race fitness on the gallops and hence the first race back after a break forms part of the training programme. However, this brings into question whether the horse is trying 100% to win. After all a horse which is considered to need the run is clearly not running to its best ability since it is short of peak fitness. Furthermore, the jockey is unlikely to give a partially fit horse the same ride as a fully fit animal and will tend to handle the horse more tenderly.

To support this theory that a horse may lack race fitness after a break from racing, two analyses of race performance against time between races is given in figures 3.15 and 3.16 for juvenile and non-juvenile runners.

Days Since Last Run	Number of Winners	Number of Runners	% Strike Rate
1-7	272	2096	13.0%
8-15	1042	8897	11.7%
16-21	624	5331	11.7%
22-28	412	3546	11.6%
29-56	479	4793	10.0%
57-84	98	1131	8.7%
85-200	51	756	6.7%
201+	0	6	0.0%
All	**2978**	**26556**	**11.2%**

Figure 3.15: Analysis by days since last run (juveniles)

Days Since Last Run	Number of Winners	Number of Runners	% Strike Rate
1-7	1861	15732	11.8%
8-15	3822	38607	9.9%
16-21	2048	20525	10.0%
22-28	1267	13230	9.6%
29-56	1499	16382	9.2%
57-84	377	4527	8.3%
85-200	682	8755	7.8%
201+	444	6878	6.5%
All	**12000**	**124636**	**9.6**

Figure 3.16: Analysis by days since last run (non-juveniles)

Clearly, it is preferable for the horse to have run recently, and consequently this time variable should be included in any prediction model. However, there are other factors which can be considered when evaluating the fitness credential of a runner. Firstly, some trainers seem more able at getting a horse back to peak race fitness after a period of inactivity. For example, John Gosden has an overall success rate of about 20%, however, with horses returning from a break of 100 days or more this strike rate improves to almost 24%. Clearly, John Gosden is capable of producing horses fully fit after a break from racing. In contrast David Elsworth's strike rate of approximately 11% drops to just over 4% for horses unraced for at least 100 days. In appendix A2 a list of trainers is given with their success rates for all horses and those unraced for more than 100 days.

It is possible to combine these two factors to produce an effective guide to the likely fitness of horses. The trainer's data can be categorised into four groups: unknown, poor, moderate, and good, which refer to the trainer's ability to produce a horse race fit after a break. Defining these categories is somewhat arbitrary and the chosen method in this text is to use the ratio of success rates given in appendix A2. Specifically:

$$\text{Ratio} = \frac{\text{Success rate for horses running after a break}}{\text{Success rate for all horses}}$$

Using this ratio the trainers can be classified as follows:

Trainer Classification	Rule
Good	Ratio >= 1.0
Moderate	0.5 <= Ratio < 1.0
Poor	Ratio < 0.5
Unknown	Runs of horses returning from a break < 10

Figure 3.17: Trainer classifications

Additionally, the time variable can be divided into two groups by introducing a time threshold. Horses which have raced more recently than the threshold number of races are considered to be race fit, the fitness of the remainder is considered questionable. The threshold for the following examples has been set at 57 days. Using these categories the following rules can be generated:

> *if   number of days since last run < 57*
> *then fitness is OK*

> *if   number of days since last run >= 57*
> *and   trainer's classification is good*
> *then fitness is OK*

> *if   number of days since last run >= 57*
> *and   trainer's classification is moderate*
> *then fitness is doubtful*

> *if   number of days since last run >= 57*
> *and   trainer's classification is poor or unknown*
> *then fitness is unlikely*

There are now three categories of fitness: *OK, doubtful* and *unlikely*. An analysis of these conclusions by success rate for all race types is given in figure 3.18. The horses for whom fitness is not in doubt seem to have a higher success rate than the others, with the unfit horses performing quite poorly.

Fitness Classification	Number of Winners	Number of Runners	% Strike Rate
Fitness OK	13812	133179	10.4%
Fitness doubtful	916	9869	9.3%
Fitness unlikely	1166	18013	6.5%

Figure 3.18: Analysis of fitness classification

Naturally, there are special cases. Some horses are easy to get fit and always seem to run well after a break. Information which can help isolate this type of horse is contained in the race commentaries. In each race commentary a reference is included regarding the paddock appearance of the horse. Fit horses are given the comment *looked well*, whist those in need of the race would be reported as *backward*. An analysis of previous paddock comments for a specific horse would indicate whether the horse is likely to be fit or not following a long absence for the track. In general, though, the above rules appear to classify between the three categories of fitness quite well and can be easily incorporated into forecasting models.

Improvement and Previous Success Rate

Unexpected results of horseraces can usually be explained by one or both of the following reasons: a) horses performing unaccountably poorly, and b) horses running well in advance of their public form. There are many reasons for horses running poorly, but broadly these can be categorised into two groups: unsuitable race conditions and physical disability. For instance, the horse may be unsuited by the race distance or the going, or the horse may be suffering from some illness which cannot be detected until after the race. The reverse can be said for horses running better than before. This improvement can be a result of the horse encountering ideal racing conditions for the first time, or as a consequence of physical improvement.

Younger horses, two-year-olds and three-year-olds, are improving throughout the season, due mainly to their continued physical development. However, determining which of these will improve more than usual is not an easy task. Fortunately, help is available via the published ratings. Both Raceform and Timeform supplement their ratings with indicators to alert the subscriber to the probable improvement likely from some animals. Raceform use a "+" symbol, whereas Timeform use a "p" to indicate that greater than normal improvement is likely, and a "P" to flag horses which they believe are definitely capable of better. The horses most likely to show improved form are those which are difficult to rate. For example, unexposed animals which have only raced a few times, or those which are unbeaten. Unbeaten animals are difficult to rate because an assumption of the superiority over the other runners needs to be made since a horse of this type has not necessarily been fully extended. Horses with the potential to improve on previous ratings need to be considered very carefully and would normally be selected over horses with similar race credentials but without the same degree of potential. In a study of non-juvenile pattern races it was found that the success rate for improving horses was 1.8 times greater than for all other runners.

The previous success rate of an animal (i.e. the number of times the horse has won compared to the number of times it has raced) is linked to improvement. Specifically, a previous success rate of 100% indicates that the horse is as yet unbeaten which is one of the criteria given for potential improvement. However, it also shows whether a horse is capable of winning a reasonable proportion of races. In figures 3.19 and 3.20 the success rate for horses with differing historical strike rates is presented. From these tables it can be seen that the likelihood of success in a race can be predicted by the previous success rate, and therefore, this component can prove useful in the development of forecasting systems.

Previous Success Rate	Number of Winners	Number of Runners	% Strike Rate
0..10%	1988	19793	10.0%
11..20%	208	2014	10.3%
21..30%	136	1158	11.7%
31..40%	183	1319	13.9%
41..50%	235	1251	18.8%
51..60%	10	59	16.9%
61..70%	47	219	21.5%
71..80%	11	41	26.8%
81..90%	0	0	-
90..100%	160	702	22.8%
All	**2978**	**26556**	**11.2%**

Figure 3.19: Analysis of previous success rate for juveniles

Previous Success Rate	Number of Winners	Number of Runners	% Strike Rate
0..10%	2988	38433	7.8%
11..20%	1988	19034	10.4%
21..30%	728	5716	12.7%
31..40%	340	2393	14.2%
41..50%	174	1127	15.4%
51..60%	19	111	17.1%
61..70%	30	166	18.1%
71..80%	10	52	19.2%
81..90%	2	8	25.0%
90..100%	62	255	24.3%
All	**6341**	**67295**	**9.4%**

Figure 3.20: Analysis of previous success rate for non-juveniles

Trainer

In similar fashion to the other critical variables, there are several approaches to representing the importance of the trainer in the forecasting model. Naturally, these methods vary in degrees of complexity, and an appropriate approach based on the availability of data and time constraints should be selected. The most straightforward approach uses a simple categorisation of the trainers based on their average success rate over a specified period of time (i.e. one or two seasons). This information is published each year in the formbook. For instance, the trainers could be divided into three groups: *Top Class*, *Good*, and *Moderate*. Success rate thresholds can be selected to discriminate between the three classes and the trainers assigned accordingly.

On a slightly more detailed level, the classes can be derived for each race type or each course. However, there are drawbacks with these approaches,

Analysis of:	H R A CECIL				Average = 307/1372 22.4%			
	All 3yo+ Runners				**3yo+ Favourites**			
By Race Type	Wins	Runs	%	AvRet	Wins	Runs	%	AvRet
Group	32	183	17.5	-0.17	14	49	28.6	-0.39
Listed	25	131	19.1	-0.33	16	38	42.1	0.01
Stakes	64	251	25.5	-0.12	34	89	38.2	-0.18
Claimers	1	2	50.0	0.75	0	1	0.0	-1.00
Maidens	141	501	28.1	0.00	89	178	50.0	0.01
Handicaps	44	304	14.5	-0.17	18	72	25.0	-0.14
First Run	36	195	18.5	0.02	18	40	45.0	-0.05
First Hcp Run	13	106	12.3	-0.33	4	25	16.0	-0.57
By position on last run: non-handicaps								
Won	50	210	23.8	-0.15	**Unraced for > 100 days**			
Second/Third	104	307	33.9	-0.03	4	24	16.7	-0.09h
Other	109	551	19.8	-0.11	32	175	18.3	-0.30n
Top 3 Tracks					**Favourite on latest run**			
Beverley	10	21	48%	0.44	20	92	21.7	0.31h
Pontefract	13	36	36%	0.22	94	287	32.8	0.04n
Ripon	15	43	35%	-0.10				

†The letters *h* and *n* next to the return denote handicap and non-handicap races.

Figure 3.21: An example analysis of trainer's success rate

notably the number of observations decreases as the level of detail increases reducing the reliability of the resultant statistics. Consequently, it may be necessary to analyse several seasons' data to generate adequate sample sizes. A more detailed analysis is given in figure 3.21, which includes winners to runners strike rate and the average return for £1 placed to win on each runner. This analysis can also be produced for individual courses, although for modelling purposes this extreme level of detail may not be necessary.

Whichever representation is chosen, an indication of the trainer's success rate should be considered before building a forecasting model. This is especially important for horses with little public form, and hence, ability ratings with low degrees of reliability.

As well as including seasonal success rates for trainers, it is also useful to consider the performance of a trainer's runners in the preceding few weeks.

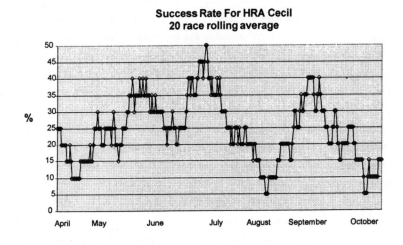

Figure 3.22: Analysis of trainer's strike rate by month

Any stable can have good and bad runs of form. A high success rate indicates that the horses are in peak physical fitness and are running to form.

A poor run with a low success rate may indicate that all is not well with the stable and some of the horses may have contracted a virus. In figure 3.22 an analysis of the success rate for the trainer Henry Cecil is given in graphical form for the 1997 season. These data are presented as rolling 20 run averages. Clearly, the horses were running well at the end of June and early July with a strike rate approaching 50%, however this exceptional performance is not continued through into August which sees a marked dip in the performance measure. Although there appears to be a revival in form in September, the season ends on a downward trend. When analysing this type of data other factors need to be considered. For instance, during the poor run at the end of the season, the horses may have been encountering better than expected opposition, or were being entered in races with large numbers of runners thus reducing their chance of success.

Jockey

In 1972 Lester Piggott won the Epsom Derby on Roberto. It was one of the closest recorded finishes of the premier Classic with Roberto winning by the narrowest margin: a short head in racing terms, 4 inches imperial. There was no doubting that Piggott was the best jockey riding in Britain, probably the best in the world, and it was remarked at the time that no other jockey would have won on Roberto that day. But what makes one jockey better than another, and how can the jockey's ability be incorporated into a forecasting model?

Like trainers, assessing the ability of jockeys is not easy. A simple analysis of a jockey's success rate can be misleading since jockeys are often linked to particular stables, so those connected with the more popular trainers will ride the better horses and should, therefore, have a higher than average winners to runners ratio. One method of categorisation, which does not attempt to assess ability, is to simply partition the jockeys by experience. In other words, to assign the jockeys to different groups depending on the number of previous rides they have had, the assumption being that more experienced jockeys should be able to use this greater experience to good effect. In the data set used to define the model, a simple indicator would identify the category to which each jockey was assigned. For instance, jockeys could be divided into three groups, top class, good and moderate, which could be represented by three inputs in the model.

An alternative approach is to assess the jockeys on their performances in close finishes. Figure 3.23 presents the success rate for several jockeys in close finishes (where a close finish is a difference of only a *head* or less between the first and second horses). A close finish indicates that the horses are equally matched, thus removing the trainers bias previously mentioned, and, in theory, the better jockey should prevail.

Jockey	Wins in Close Finishes	Number of Close Finishes	Success Rate %
Pat Eddery	17	23	73.9%
C Lowther	7	11	63.6%
T Quinn	7	11	63.6%
P Fessey	8	13	61.5%
Dane O'Neill	11	18	61.1%
R Hills	11	18	61.1%
R Ffrench	12	20	60.0%
T Sprake	9	15	60.0%
J Fortune	13	22	59.1%
Paul Eddery	6	11	54.5%
R Cochrane	9	17	52.9%
Martin Dwyer	10	19	52.6%
M Hills	10	19	52.6%
L Dettori	20	39	51.3%
K Fallon	20	40	50.0%
S Drowne	5	10	50.0%
W Ryan	10	20	50.0%
J Reid	13	27	48.1%
J F Egan	9	19	47.4%
M Fenton	7	15	46.7%
K Darley	16	35	45.7%
G Carter	5	11	45.5%
J Weaver	9	20	45.0%
G Duffield	10	23	43.5%
M Roberts	6	14	42.9%
J Carroll	7	17	41.2%
L Charnock	7	17	41.2%
C Rutter	4	10	40.0%
J Quinn	5	14	35.7%
D Holland	7	21	33.3%
S Sanders	9	29	31.0%
A Clark	4	14	28.6%
A Culhane	5	18	27.8%
R Hughes	3	12	25.0%

Figure 3.23: Analysis of close finishes

From figure 3.23 it would appear that Pat Eddery is the best jockey in a close finish, and of those analysed, Richard Hughes the weakest. However, the vast majority (22 of the 32 jockeys) have success rates in the 40%-60% range which, given an expected success rate of 50%, indicates very little difference between the riders. And in fact, in 1972 when Lester Piggott was riding with such effect he only managed a success rate of 60% in close finishes.

Although this approach results in an ordered list of jockeys, there is a problem with the method. It is assumed that all jockeys race against each other with equal frequencies. For Pat Eddery, for instance, this would mean that the distribution of his rides against all other jockeys is uniform. In other words, he would ride against Chris Rutter as many times as he would against Richard Hills. However, this is not necessarily true. Those jockeys thought to be better by trainers and owners tend to ride in the more prestigious races and at the main race meetings of the day (i.e. the meeting with the most prize-money). Consequently, Pat Eddery is more likely to race against Lanfranco Dettori than, Lindsay Charnock for instance. Although Lindsay Charnock is an exceptionally talented jockey, he would be unlikely to ride at all the main meetings, the majority of which are in southern England, since he is not connected with a major owner or stable, and rides mainly in the north of the country. This unreliable assumption probably explains the relatively low positions of Dettori and Fallon in the table, possibly the two best jockeys currently riding.

A more complete analysis can be based on an independent measure of performance. In previous sections the starting price has been used as this independent measure of probable success. However, when considering jockeys, the starting price is no longer independent since the presence of a top jockey will depress the animal's odds. Ratings, though, are independent of jockey. A top jockey will not effect the rating given to a horse since this measure is determined from historical race performances and does not include current race factors except weight carried. Consequently, by restricting the analysis of jockeys' rides by rating, the better jockeys should ride a higher proportion of winners. Figure 3.24 presents this analysis for horses top rated on speed figures. For the sample of races taken (over 3,000) the average success rate for top-rated horses was 16%, consequently any jockey with a success rate exceeding 16% could be said to be performing better than average.

Jockey	Rides	%
L Dettori	66	56.1
K Fallon	80	48.8
G Duffield	34	35.3
J Weaver	46	30.4
M Hills	38	28.9
M Roberts	39	25.6
D Holland	44	25.0
Pat Eddery	65	24.6
K Darley	66	24.2
L Charnock	34	23.5
A Clark	47	23.4
Paul Eddery	30	23.3
G Carter	31	22.6
Dean McKeown	45	22.2
Dane O'Neill	42	21.4
J Reid	59	20.3
W Ryan	35	20.0
Martin Dwyer	58	19.0
R Cochrane	58	19.0
R Ffrench	77	18.2
F Lynch	36	16.7
S Sanders	65	15.4
R Hills	39	15.4
A Culhane	34	14.7
R Winston	41	14.6
G Bardwell	42	14.3
T Williams	38	13.2
J Carroll	39	12.8
T Sprake	33	12.1
S Drowne	50	12.0
S Whitworth	34	11.8
J Fortune	52	11.5
Iona Wands	36	11.1
R Mullen	48	10.4
D Wright	30	10.0
N Carlisle	30	10.0
T Quinn	52	9.6
C Rutter	33	9.1
J Bramhill	82	8.5
P Fessey	53	7.5
J Quinn	91	6.6
A Daly	49	6.1
N Adams	44	4.5
Expected	-	*16.0*

Figure 3.24: Jockeys' success rate on top rated horses

Figure 3.24 is very different from figure 3.23, with those jockeys thought to be the best, Dettori and Fallon, moving from mid-table to the top with success rates exceeding 45%. Using an expanded version of this table, covering more riders, it is possible to partition the jockeys into groups for use in the model itself. Alternatively the success rate itself could be used.

Summary

Evaluating the profile of a horse is not necessarily straightforward, however, it is very important. The profile provides the information on which the race forecast will be made by converting the raw data of race performances into a meaningful summary of the animal's like, dislikes and ability, amongst other things. In this chapter several components of the profile have been considered and methods to evaluate them proposed. However, these attributes are not the only relevant factors and others could equally well have been considered, suitability of the course configuration for example. Furthermore, the methods developed to evaluate these factors are only *suggested* approaches, many others will exist in varying degrees of complexity and will possibly generate better results. It is distinctly possible that minor modifications to the proposed methods will provide more accurate evaluations. Adjusting the thresholds used in the evaluation of fitness for example, may prove beneficial. Similarly, including other information such as pedigrees may improve the assessment of such factors as going and distance suitability. Whether it is decided to adopt the rules illustrated in this chapter or generate a modified set, evaluating the profile of the horse is a critical stage in the forecasting model and should be examined very closely.

References

[1] *Flat Racing For Profit*, by P. J. May, published by Raceform, Newbury, Berks, 1996.
[2] *Horse Race Betting and Selection*, by P. Braddock, Longman Group Limited, England, 1983.
[3] *Betting For A Living*, by N. Mordin, Aesculus Press, England, 1992.
[4] *Jump Racing For Profit*, by P. J. May, published by Raceform, Newbury, Berks, 1996.

4

Probabilities and Profit

This chapter explores the differences between selecting winners and determining profitable betting options. Whilst, at first, there may appear to be no difference between these two concepts, it is not always the case that the most likely winner of a race offers the best possible bet. The probability, or degree of belief, of success for each runner is the most important output of any forecasting model since it allows the bettor to make a comparison with the prices on offer. Consequently, the formulation of these probabilities constitutes a crucial part of the race forecasting exercise. This chapter starts with an examination of different forms of the forecasting model before investigating methods for generating probabilistic outputs.

Forecasting Objectives

The design of any forecasting model is of paramount importance. In the previous chapter the key components for evaluating each runner were analysed, however no reference was made to the general design of the model. Before creating the model the question of within race competition needs to be addressed. One solution is to construct one input pattern for each race i.e. to list all the attributes for each horse in a single pattern. However, two further problems are created with this approach. Firstly, the number of runners in each race varies from two to over thirty and as a consequence the input patterns will contain many missing fields. Secondly, the number of variables becomes difficult to handle. Although only a relatively small number of elements are deemed important for race analysis, representing these concepts for all horses in a race would produce an extremely large input data set and severely complicate model building. For example, representing the profile of each horse with only twelve variables would produce a race-model with 360 inputs to cover a 30 runner race.

The second approach is to use one pattern per horse and forecast the likely finishing position of the horse, addressing the within race competition as part of a second phase of modelling. This method was also adopted by Chen *et al*[1] when modelling Greyhound racing. In this case the data file would be structured as in figure 4.1 where the independent variables represent the animal's profile and are used to predict the dependent variable (also referred to as the target variable).

Horse: 1	Profile	Finishing Position
Horse: 2	Profile	Finishing Position
⋮	⋮	⋮
Horse: n	Profile	Finishing Position
Record Id.	*Independent Vars.*	*Dependent Var.*

Figure 4.1: File structure

There are several ways in which the discrimination between winners and losers can be made and the *finishing position* in figure 4.1 represented. Firstly, the obvious categorisation concerns the finishing position which can be represented with a binary variable, specifically one for those horses which win and zero for the remainder, or as a ratio of the number of runners in the race. A second discriminating variable is the distance a horse is beaten by the winner (zero for a winner). Such a model would forecast the likely distance beaten for each horse in the race, the likely winner being the horse with the lowest predicted value. A third method of classification concerns the use of race times. The target variable of this model would be the time each horse takes to run the race, again the likely winner would be the horse with the lowest predicted time. The chosen representation depends on the type of model intended. Once the model has been created the within race competition can be considered with a process that normalises for the effect of multiple runners.

Is Finding the Winner Enough?

Whilst developing forecasting methods for predicting the likely outcome of horseraces is an interesting theoretical exercise, with respect to betting it is only a part of the solution. In order to return a long-term profit from betting on horses it is not only necessary to have reliable methods of predicting race results, but to be able to identify profitable bets by associating a probability with each prediction that can be compared to the prices offered by the bookmakers.

To quantify the task of profitable betting, selecting a horse at random would return a loss of approximately 30p for every £1 staked. Add to this the cost of off-course betting tax at 9% and the total loss becomes about 40p per £1 staked. Therefore, the bettor needs to develop methods which can turn a 40p loss into a profit, which is no simple task. Interestingly, though, this task compares quite favourably to some other forms of betting. For instance the National Lottery returns only 50p per £1 staked (i.e. a loss to the bettor of 50p per £1 staked). However, compared to the stock market, possibly the most popular form of gambling, horseracing offers a very poor return. The stock market is by far the best bet since even by selecting a share portfolio at random the expected long-term profit is positive.

Players of Roulette expect a return of just over 97p for every £1 staked. So perhaps this is a better betting medium than horseracing. Well, although the return per bet is significantly higher, the chance of making a long term profit is negligible. This is a result of the randomness of the game. In Roulette, or any numbers game of this type such as lotteries (including the 49's daily draw), the outcome of each spin of the wheel or selection of a number is entirely random. Due to this randomness it is not possible to predict with any confidence the outcome of each event but it is possible to predict accurately the *probability* of every outcome. For instance the probability of the ball in roulette landing on a red segment of the wheel is 18/37, since there are 18 red, 18 black, and one green segments. Consequently, the odds on offer can be tailored to suit this expectation and ensure that the house makes a profit. Hence the 3p loss. The randomness means that the bettor is unable to turn this loss into a profit since there are no methods for predicting the outcome of the next spin with any degree of certainty. Horseracing, on the other hand, is not entirely random, and it is not possible to determine *exactly* the probability of any one horse winning any one race (walkovers excepted).

This level of uncertainty means that different estimates of probabilities will exist between bettors and bookmakers. Consequently, it is possible to improve one's likelihood of success by more accurately assessing the probabilities, and ultimately make a profit.

Probability Estimates

There are two distinct approaches to generating forecasting methods which aim to generate profit as opposed to selecting winners. The first uses the return variable as the dependent variable in the model itself. In other words instead of predicting likely finishing position, for instance, the model will aim to predict the likely return for a fixed unit stake. This approach is used in Chapter 5 when rule-based methods are considered. The second approach is to predict a race dependent variable such as finishing position or race time and then to apply some normalising criterion to convert this output to probabilities of success, and ultimately to odds. This method is preferable when races are to be analysed on an individual basis, with model predictions converted to odds to determine whether a bet should be placed. The former method is more applicable to methods which generate general relationships (such as rules) which can be applied without specific reference to all race details.

Adjusting the forecasting method to predict likely return is a relatively straightforward task with the return variable incorporated into the model. However, long priced winners should be treated carefully since they can have a significant effect on the model. The second approach, though, is slightly more complex and is considered in detail in the following sections.

The output from the forecasting models will normally be a numeric value on some pre-determined scale depending on which dependent variable is chosen. For instance, the values may lie between 0 and 1 for models which aim to discriminate between winners and the remainder of runners. This output is referred to in the remainder of this chapter as the *model output*. One model output is associated with each runner. Naturally the horse with the highest (or lowest in the case of race times) model output would be considered the most likely winner of the race. However, in isolation, this model output does not represent a probability of success since the actual chance of winning is dependent on all the runners in the race. For instance, a horse with a model output of 80 would have a better chance of winning a race with only one opponent rated, say, 60 than it would against four other horses rated between 70 and 75. Ideally this model output should be converted to a scale which accounts for the within race competition and expresses the chance of success in the form of odds.

In order to illustrate methods for converting model outputs to probabilities, a previously published model[2] will be used as an example. This example uses a knowledge-based approach (see Chapter 6) to predict the results of non-juvenile Listed races. The model was tested on all non-juvenile Listed races run over five seasons from 1987-91. The output of the knowledge-base is a figure on a scale of 50 to 100 for each runner. An analysis of these outputs is given in figure 4.2.

Model Output	Winners	Runners	Success Rate %
50..64	3	28	10.7
64..66	1	41	2.4
66..68	8	106	7.5
68..70	12	203	5.9
70..72	36	363	9.9
72..74	66	398	16.6
74..76	57	297	19.2
76..78	46	157	29.3
78..100	47	136	34.6
All	**276**	**1729**	**16.0**

Figure 4.2: Output of knowledge-based model for Listed races

From figure 4.2 it can be seen that a reasonably strong correlation exists between the model outputs and the winners to runner success ratio. In other words the model is performing quite well. This relationship is more clearly presented in graphical form (figure 4.3).

The process of converting the model outputs to odds requires a relationship to be determined between the model outputs themselves and the likelihood of success. Such a relationship would ideally be monotonically increasing so that the derived probability of success increases as the model output

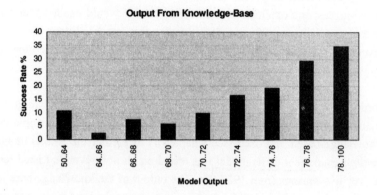

Figure 4.3: Graph of model outputs

increases. Additionally, it should be positive for any model output value since the concept of negative odds is difficult to resolve. However, there are problems associated with this task of eliciting theoretical probabilities from sample data frequencies. In the text Probabilistic Causality[3], Ellery Eells asserts that the real world may contain "mere accidental coincidences" which can result in frequencies that misrepresent the causal facts, and that therefore do not allow probability to reflect the causal facts in a natural way. This is clearly more relevant in small samples, and is illustrated in the Listed race problem by the abnormally high winners to runners success rate exhibited by horses rated less than 64. It is therefore important to construct a model that not only mirrors the sample data but also reflects the real world situation.

Intuitively, the model should possess a form similar to that displayed by a logistic curve (figure 4.4). The logistic function is identified by the equation

$$f(x) = \frac{1}{1 + e^{(b_0 + b_1 x)}}$$

where the parameters b_0 and b_1 are derived from the sample data.

The logistic function has three valuable properties for this particular application. Firstly, it remains positive for all values of the model output, secondly, it is monotonically increasing, and thirdly, the gradient reduces

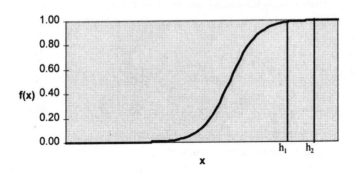

General Form of the Logistic Curve

Figure 4.4: A logistic curve

rapidly at the extremes. The requirement for the first two properties has already been mentioned, however the necessity for the third requires more explanation. There may be cases when the model output assumes an extremely high value, say h_1, and as such the probability of failure would be considered to be negligible. In the horseracing problem, the only conceivable means of defeat would be by accident, for instance falling. Similarly, a value h_2 may equally be assigned to an event, where h_2 is larger than h_1. In this instance the probability of success is not materially increased because the *accident factor*, constituting the majority of the probability of failure, is independent of h_i and, hence, the probability of success (i.e. the value tending towards $1-p$(accident)) would be only marginally effected for such extreme cases. Consequently, a constant rate of change would misrepresent the probability of success. Likewise, a similar argument would also hold for exceptionally low h_i values where the only conceivable chance of success depends upon a failing of the opposition due to the accident factor producing a freak result. A function which maintained a relatively steep gradient at these extremes, as in the case of a straight line, would not accurately reflect the true changes in probabilities.

Although the logistic curve can be used to estimate the success ratio for the model outputs associated with a single horse, it does not completely account for the within race competition. To solve this problem it is necessary to normalise the derived probability estimates such that their aggregate equals

73

one. This is a simple procedure merely requiring each probability to be divided by the sum of probabilities for all horses in the race. The resultant normalised ratios represent the probability of success for each horse in the race. It is then a straightforward task to convert these probabilities to odds, thus providing an effective means of supporting the model output associated with each runner.

As an illustration of this technique, consider the following model outputs for a four runner race given in figure 4.5. Since the logistic curve is monotonically increasing, the highest probability of success is associated with the highest model output, namely 75. And in this case, the probability, when normalised, is equivalent to odds of $^{11}/_{10}$. Consequently, a price of $^{11}/_{10}$ or higher would appear to offer a good betting opportunity for this horse.

Model Output	Logistic Value	Normalised Probability	Fair Odds
75	0.175	0.472	11/10
65	0.089	0.241	3/1
60	0.063	0.169	5/1
55	0.043	0.117	15/2

Figure 4.5: Calculation of odds

The generation of odds in this way is more acceptable in the horseracing environment than many others simply because the user may make comparisons with the price on offer by the bookmakers and adjust the bet type, or stake, accordingly. In weather forecasting, for example, knowing in advance that the probability of rain is 40% rather than 20% is difficult to interpret and use to the best effect. Would one always carry an umbrella if the probability of rain is greater than zero, or would the percentage need to be larger than some other arbitrary value, say 75%? However, in horseracing, the investor is able to vary the amount staked from zero to his/her limit and respond to the probabilities more directly. In this respect, the odds do not represent the likelihood of success, but offer a measure of confidence in the forecaster's methodology.

References

[1] *Expert Prediction, Symbolic Learning, and Neural Networks: An Experiment on Greyhound Racing*, by H. Chen, P. B. Rinde, L. She, S. Sutjaho, C. Sommer and D. Neely, in IEEE Expert, December 1994.

[2] *The Application of Expert Systems to Forecasting*, by P. J. Howes, Master of Philosophy Degree Thesis, School of Computing and Mathematical Sciences, Oxford Brookes University, 1993.

[3] *Probabilistic Causality*, by E. Eells, Cambridge, England: CUP, 1991.

5

The Rule-Based Approach

The earlier chapters of this book have summarised the necessary background information relating to the horseracing problem, in this chapter the first forecasting methods are proposed. Rule-based methods, discussed in the following sections, are very easy to implement and can prove to be very effective at returning a profit and, consequently, are worthy of serious consideration when forming a comprehensive betting strategy. Unlike many forecasting models which attempt to predict the results of races, the aim of the following rule-based approaches is to maximise the return (i.e. the profit) and hence a detailed examination of the starting prices and probabilities of success is not necessary since any horse which satisfies the rules of the system is, by definition, a value bet.

Rule-Based Systems

Humans use rules to govern many aspects of life. At national level rules, or laws, are created to provide the population with specific bounds and to maintain acceptable living conditions. At individual level, we apply rules all the time, whether it is in regard to our weekly shopping requirement or the time we need to leave home each day to reach work by an agreed time. Although when considering the laws of a country we would no doubt refer to them as rules, at the individual level we may not think of many of our decisions as being rule-based. This is simply because we have become *experts* in everyday life. Experts can intuitively see what the consequences of an action will be and what needs to be done in order for a particular outcome to be achieved. Consequently, we see an empty coffee jar and note the fact that more coffee should be purchased. As an example of the effect of expertise, consider a receptionist on his/her first day at work. The senior member of staff detailed to instruct the new recruit may inform him/her that when the telephone rings it should be answered within a set time (i.e. three rings) and the enquirer greeted in a specific way. The novice receptionist, therefore, is thinking: *if* the telephone rings *then* I must pick it up within three rings and say .... This is rule following. However, a few days later answering the telephone in this specific manner has become *natural* to the receptionist who would no longer be conscious of following a set of *if..then..* style rules.

In horserace prediction rule-based methods (or systems) are very popular. Most bettors have their own systems to follow in addition to form study. For example, some bettors will look for specific jockey/trainer combinations or bet horses which have travelled over a certain distance to the track. In rule form these methods would be:

> *if   Jockey A is riding*
> *and horse is trained by Trainer B*
> *then bet*

> *if   distance travelled from stable to racecourse exceeds n miles*
> *then bet*

There are two main advantages with these methods: they are precisely structured and are easy to apply. Their rigid style allows for easy testing against known race results and the bettor can soon deduce whether a rule is worth following. Simplicity is important for many bettors who have little time to study form and in this regard rules can often be applied in a few minutes. However, there are disadvantages with these approaches. For instance, the rigidity of the rule does not always sanction for changing circumstances, nor exceptional conditions. As an example, rules involving trainers do not allow for periods of poor stable form which may be the result of a virus affecting the health of the stable's runners. Notwithstanding the problems associated with rules, in this chapter three rule-based methods are discussed following a brief summary of guidelines for developing rule-based methods.

Developing Rule-Based Systems for Horseracing

There are an infinite number of racing systems. However, only a small percentage will return the bettor a profit, and an even smaller number will be both profitable and reliable. The following guidelines, which were first published in a slightly modified form in *Jump Racing For Profit* (Raceform, 1996), will hopefully provide a basis for system development.

Simplicity - When designing a selection method it is important not to make it too complex. As the number of variables increases (i.e. distance beaten last time, going last time, going today, race distance last time, race distance today, days since last run etc.) the amount of data needed to give meaningful test results increases. Complex systems are also difficult to implement, requiring a great deal of searching through previous form to determine the selection.

Uniqueness - Try to find *new* relationships between the data. Using the normal data items in conventional fashion will, in all probability, produce losing systems. The odds on offer account for the established trends, and consequently there is no value for the punter.

Logic - When searching for unique approaches it is imperative to ensure that the variables used are sensible. For instance, whilst backing all horses ridden by bearded jockeys may have returned a profit in the past, facial hair can hardly be considered a reliable discriminating factor with regard to the chances of racing success.

Correlation - Be wary of ill-founded relationships and hidden correlations. As an example, horses running in August tend to produce faster race times than those running in March, therefore they must be better animals. Whilst this conclusion seems a logical deduction from the available evidence, it is an unconsidered variable which produces this result, namely the going. Faster going produces faster race times and the ground is likely to ride firmer in August than March, hence the faster times.

Measurement - Base the selection methods on quantifiable variables, for example data items such as the historical wins to runs success rate of the horse. Try to avoid qualitative items such as suitability of going, distance etc., unless these terms can be defined precisely. Opinion is difficult to analyse, and it is far from constant.

Data Collection - There are three issues concerned with data collection: quality, quantity and spread. Clearly, the data collected needs to be accurate and unbiased. This seems obvious, but it is not necessarily a straightforward task to undertake, especially when extracting data manually from a formbook. It is very easy to omit particular races during the extraction process reasoning: 'Well, I wouldn't have bet in that race anyway'. Naturally, sufficient data needs to be collected to support the complexity of the system, however, too many seasons' data can introduce bias due to the ongoing changing nature of racing. Paradoxically, it is not advisable to extract data from just one season. Certain conditions of the year, weather, quality of horse etc., will bias any analysis. The data needs to be spread evenly over a few recent seasons.

Strike rate - Aim for an approach with a reasonable winner to bets strike rate. A strike rate of just 10% is not really high enough, the losing runs will occur too frequently and could be extremely long (see *Running The System*). Aim for a strike rate of at least 20%.

Testing - There are two different ways of testing a new selection method. The first involves partitioning the data set *before* the development process. One part can be used for development and the other for testing. For instance, if the data have been collected from four seasons, the first three seasons could be used to develop and refine the system with the fourth season used for testing. The second method is to test the system live. In other words, develop the approach on all available and relevant data, and conduct the testing phase during the following year by either keeping a record of the system's performance or by actually backing the selections to small stakes. In addition to providing a real test environment, this approach is also one of education for the bettor. By closely monitoring the system through the placement of bets, the bettor will get a better *feel* for the method and perhaps identify other highly correlated variables. For instance the likelihood of long losing runs, the way he/she reacts after several losing bets etc. Once satisfied with the validity of the system the punter can then increase the stakes.

Running The System - It is very easy to break the rules of the system, especially during long losing runs. This behaviour should be avoided.

Providing the system has been based on well-founded ideas, and has been adequately tested, there is no need to doubt its ability to return a profit. Consequently, the devised staking plan should be adhered to. There is nothing worse than finding, at the end of the year, that you have lost money, and that if you had kept to the system's rules you would have made a profit.

In the following section the guidelines listed above will be used to develop three rule-based approaches which will hopefully return a profit.

Selected Rule-Based Methods

Whilst *profitable systems*, of various degrees of merit, are advertised for sale in every horseracing publication, very little research of an academic nature has been published on the subject. Dayan and McCartney[1] have published the results of six models they developed which were applicable to American horseracing. They concluded that, whilst it is possible to develop predictive models for horseracing, 'it is hard to believe that there is a way to beat the system significantly'. In contrast to these findings, Roger Vergin tested six previously published rule-based methods and reported his results in *An Investigation of Decision Rules for Thoroughbred Race Horse Wagering*[2]. These systems had been developed by several other researchers, and included such information as the winning percentage of each runner, speed ratings, weight carried and days since last outing. All of which have been analysed in Chapter 3. After extensive testing, Vergin concluded that 'the systematic evaluation of horseracing data might lead to the development of a profitable betting system'.

The following methods are based on similar approaches to the systems evaluated by Vergin and use the conclusions derived in Chapter 3. The first system is applicable to juvenile horses (i.e. horses aged two years old) whilst the other two methods are relevant to non-juvenile races. The data used to develop these methods covered the seasons 1994 to 1997, and they are evaluated using 1998 data. For convenience, the return is expressed as a proportion of a £1 stake, excluding tax. Therefore, an average return of 0.25 for a number of bets equates to a profit of 25p for each £1 staked per bet. A negative figure naturally indicates a loss. When expressing return as an average for a number of bets, the lower limit is bounded at -1.00 which implies no winners from the sample of bets. In other words a loss of £1 for every £1 staked. The upper limit is unbounded, although an average return of more than 0.09 indicates an profit after tax, and it is very unlikely that this figure will exceed 0.50 for a reasonably sized sample of bets.

Method 1: Juvenile Favourites

A great deal of information can be learned from a two-year-old's first career run. The race distance, time of year, choice of racecourse and starting price all provide valuable information about the horse. For example, a two-year-old horse making its debut in the early Spring will need to be a sharp, precocious animal with plenty of speed. These horses are likely to be run over sprint distances throughout their careers and will probably fall short of Group 1 class. A juvenile starting its career over, say, 7 furlongs is likely to become a middle distance horse the following season. The more backward two-year-old horses will not make their debuts until late in the season, possibly September or October, and are likely to make much better three-year-olds than juveniles, normally making significant physical development over the winter months. However, of all the factors surrounding a two-year-old's debut probably the most important is its starting price. The better two-year-old runners are known well in advance of racing by bookmakers and the racing public alike, and as a result start at quite short prices. Figure 5.1 presents the distribution of horses making their juvenile debuts by starting price, it also shows the average return per £1 staked on each to win.

Starting Price	Winners	Runners	Success Rate	Average Return/£1
Odds On	84	138	60.9%	0.00
Evens - 2/1	119	322	37.0%	-0.05
85/40 - 5/1	244	1190	20.5%	-0.08
11/2 - 10/1	150	1808	8.3%	-0.31
11/1 - 20/1	71	2637	2.7%	-0.56
21/1 - 40/1	27	2066	1.3%	-0.59
41/1+	3	853	0.4%	-0.82
All	**698**	**9014**	**7.7%**	**-0.45**

Figure 5.1: Analysis of juvenile debuts by starting price

From these figures it can be seen that very few high priced horses win on their debuts. In fact, only 30 horses priced at higher than $^{20}/_1$ won from almost 3,000 runners, a success rate of just over 1%. This is also reflected in the huge level stake loss of over 65p per £1 staked on these horses. Clearly, the prices of these runners are not reflecting the low probabilities of success. However, for odds on chances the success rate exceeds 60% and the loss per bet is negligible (before tax). It should be remembered that these horses have never previously raced and therefore can only be judged on breeding, appearance in the parade ring and *inside information*. This lack of prior evidence also accounts for the higher than average loss returned for all two-year-old debutants, 45p per £1 staked compared to about 30p for all runners, illustrating bookmakers' higher degree of caution when offering prices about these horses.

The question remains, though, whether this information can be combined into a profitable rule-based approach. From figure 5.1 it can be seen that by simply betting on these well regarded horses, for instance those starting at less than $^2/_1$, on their first racecourse appearance will not return a profit. However, by following these horses on their next few runs does return a profit, especially if they lose on their debuts. Although this seems paradoxical, following horses which under-perform on their debuts, it exploits the over-pricing associated with these horses in their subsequent runs, thus producing a betting opportunity. It is equivalent to a casino changing the odds on each number on the roulette wheel simply due to the weight of money staked and the recent frequency distribution of winning numbers. Providing the wheel is not biased, the underlying probability of success for each number has not changed, therefore some would be under-priced and some over-priced as a result of the changes. Consequently, some numbers would offer a viable betting proposition.

Converting these findings into a rule is a simple task requiring only the definition of a well regarded horse. In this example, the definition becomes all two-year-old horses which start at evens or less for their debuts in fields of 7 or more runners. In rule form:

> *if   the two-year-old is making its debut*
> *and   the number of runners is 7 or more*
> *and   its starting price is evens or less*
> *then   two-year-old is well regarded*

An analysis of the subsequent performance of *well regarded* juveniles resulted in the following rule-based method:

>*if*   *the two-year-old is well regarded*
>*and*   *was beaten on its first run*
>*then*   *back it to win on its next two runs*

Over the four seasons 1994-97 using this rule would have resulted in a total of 61 bets of which 27 were successful, just over 44%. The profit per £1 staked was a little over 38p.

It was mentioned that choice of racecourse for a two-year-old's first run provides important information for the race analyst, with the most important course being Newmarket. Often referred to as the home of Flat racing, Newmarket generally stages highly competitive juvenile races, especially in the latter part of the season. Consequently, any two-year-old making its debut and starting favourite for a race at Newmarket is likely to be above average. Again, using the principle regarding horses losing on their debuts, a rule can be formed as follows:

>*if*   *two-year-old was a beaten favourite at Newmarket on its debut*
>*then*   *back it to win on its next run*

During the four test seasons this rule produced 12 winners from 24 bets (50% success rate) and a level stake profit of 23p per £1 staked.

Both of these rules appear to satisfy the guidelines discussed earlier. For example, both are relatively simple to use, possess a degree of logic, are not ambiguous in definition and satisfy the lower bounds of success rate and return rate. Neither of the rules are exclusively based on a particular trainer or jockey, and would only be seriously affected if trainers suddenly changed their approach to running their better two-year-olds. Consequently, there is no reason to expect these rules not to perform equally as well in the future.

Method 2: 100% Success Rate

This rule-based approach is applicable to non-juvenile horses only. In Chapter 3 the importance of previous success rate of horses was discussed in relation to predicting the most likely winner of a race. Figure 3.20 which analysed runners by previous success rate is reproduced in this section with an additional column showing average return per bet.

Previous Success Rate	Number of Winners	Number of Runners	Success Rate %	Average Return/£1
0..10%	2988	38433	7.8%	-0.37
11..20%	1988	19034	10.4%	-0.23
21..30%	728	5716	12.7%	-0.21
31..40%	340	2393	14.2%	-0.17
41..50%	174	1127	15.4%	-0.26
51..60%	19	111	17.1%	-0.07
61..70%	30	166	18.1%	-0.23
71..80%	10	52	19.2%	-0.25
81..90%	2	8	25.0%	-0.68
90..100%	62	255	24.3%	+0.19
All	6341	67295	9.4%	-0.31

Figure 5.2: Analysis of previous success rate for non-juveniles

Figure 5.2 shows the near monotonically increasing relationship between the current and previous success rates. Whilst this is not unexpected, the return column shows a very different trend. The return appears to be almost uniformly distributed with respect to previous success. This is easily explained by considering the pricing policy of the bookmakers. Naturally, horses with high success rates will be more popular with bettors and hence will be returned at shorter starting prices. In other words, the previous success rate of a horse is generally accounted for in its price. However, there is one category which does return a profit, namely horses with a previous success rate of 90% or more. Therefore, it would be possible to return a profit by simply backing these horses. The winners to runners ratio, though, of just over 24% is a little on the low side and very near the lower bound of 20% quoted in the guidelines. And whist the return rate of 19p per £1 staked is acceptable it is still only 10% after tax to off-course punters.

It is possible to improve the return rate, but not the success ratio, by considering horses which have run only once, although this does reduce the total number of bets. For non-juvenile horses which have run only once and have won, the average return for the four year period 1994-97 is slightly over 24p per £1 staked. In rule form:

> *if   a non-juvenile horse has run once and won*
> *then back it to win on its next run*

Although the success ratio is on the low side at 24%, there are other advantages with this rule. Firstly, its simplicity. Identifying qualifying horses is a very simple task which does not require any formbook or specialist racing paper. Secondly, the rule is precise containing no ambiguous statements. And thirdly, it is not prone to distortion by other factors, for instance, if particular stables perform poorly during the year. Therefore, this system satisfies the guidelines and should continue to produce a profit.

Method 3: The Draw

The final rule-based method discussed in this section uses the effect of the draw. This feature of horseracing was discussed in Chapter 3 and its importance on certain racecourses was illustrated by an analysis of the draw effect at Chester. To briefly recap, starting stalls not only control the start of a race but also determine over which part of the track the horses will run. Due to the effects of watering, course configuration or the weather, horses racing on certain parts of the course will be at an advantage. Consequently, the draw determines whether a horse will race on, or near to, the preferred part of the course. In this respect the draw can have a pronounced effect on the result of races on some courses.

Naturally, this type of advantage is of most importance in races where the horses are equally matched, such as handicaps. Although handicap races are staged for juveniles, these horses are often unexposed in terms of ability and can improve significantly from race to race. Therefore, the process of handicapping does not always have the same normalising effect as it does for older, exposed, animals. Consequently non-juvenile handicaps are chosen as the race type for this rule-based method.

As mentioned in Chapter 4 there exists a difference between predicting winners and making a profit. This is clearly illustrated by this method. It may seem paradoxical, but the tracks with the greatest draw bias are not necessarily the best with respect to betting. The reason is simple: a significant draw bias is widely known by the betting public and bookmakers alike, and is accounted for in the prices offered. Consequently, the effect of the draw needs exploring in a different way from the approach taken in Chapter 3, namely in terms of expected profit. Using the concept of maximising return, discussed in the previous chapter, it is possible to determine which courses offer the best draw-based betting opportunities. The graph in figure 5.3 shows the average return from betting on each horse in 5 furlong non-juvenile handicap races at Chester, and is comparable to figure 3.14 presented earlier.

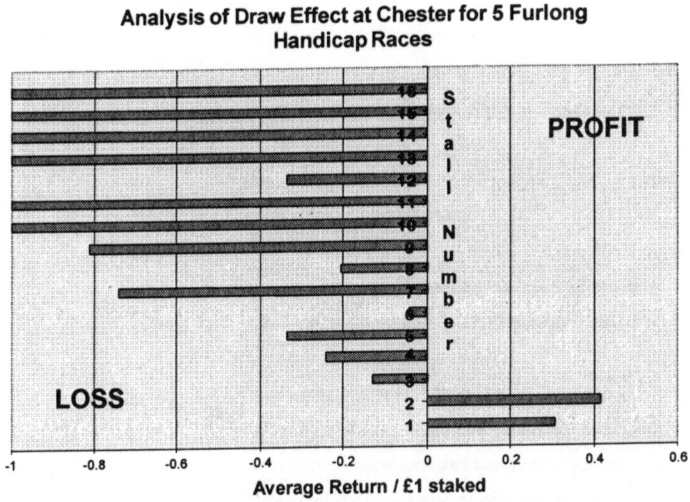

Analysis of Draw Effect at Chester for 5 Furlong Handicap Races

Figure 5.3: Analysis of the average return by stall number

From figure 3.14 it is known that there is a significant advantage to the horses drawn low which is also reflected in figure 5.3 with only two profitable stalls, namely stalls 1 and 2. The average loss of £1.00 for the higher stalls indicates that no winners were recorded in the sample from these stalls, again illustrating the importance of the draw at this particular course. The two lowest stalls recorded winners to runners success rates of 15% and 22% and average returns of 31p and 42p per £1 staked, this compares to an average strike of 10% for all runners with an average loss of 30p per £1 staked.

Although examining the profit/loss values for each stall indicates whether low drawn horses are favoured, a slight modification is required to determine whether horses drawn high are worth following. As stated in Chapter 3, a simple analysis of the horses by stall number does not account for the differences in field sizes. For instance, a horse drawn 16 will have at least 15 other horses to beat (excluding non-runners) whereas a horse drawn in stall 4 may only have three opponents, and consequently a better chance of success. To account for this effect it is necessary to adjust the stall number to a constant base before analysing the results. For example, one method is to consider the stall in relation to the highest drawn horse in the race. Therefore, in a twenty runner race stall 20 becomes stall 0, stall 19 becomes stall 1 and so on. And in an eight runner race, stall 8 becomes stall 0, stall 7 becomes stall 1 etc. The resulting analysis is then comparable to that given in figure 5.3.

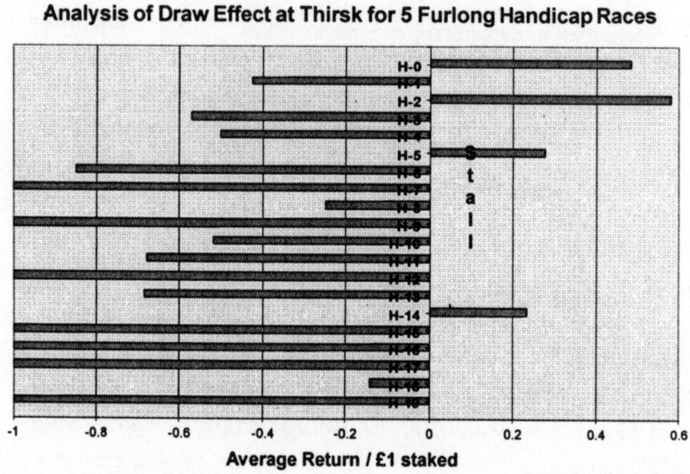

Analysis of Draw Effect at Thirsk for 5 Furlong Handicap Races

Figure 5.4: Analysis of the average return by adjusted stall number

Figure 5.4 presents a profit analysis for 5 furlong non-juvenile handicap races at Thirsk, using the modification previously discussed. Although the horses drawn high account for a high percentage of the winners (over 45% of winners are drawn in the highest three stalls) the bias is not as strong in terms of profit. This is to be expected since the draw bias at this track is well known and is hence reflected in the prices on offer about the runners.

It is distinctly possible that the profit for a particular stall is due to chance alone, or a single high priced winner. This is why a degree of care is necessary when determining which stalls to follow in the future. For instance, a profitable stall located in the centre of the track surrounded by losing stalls is unlikely to have resulted from a draw bias and therefore unlikely to reproduce the profit in the future. The *logic* section of the guidelines was included to cover this type of scenario. When analysing the draw to generate profitable betting approaches, it is preferable to concentrate on tracks where the draw bias is illustrated over several stalls, i.e. a gradually increasing or decreasing profit trend per stall. For the 5 furlong course at Chester, there is no reason to suppose that supporting horses racing from stall 12 would produce a better return than those drawn in stalls 11 or 13, however, from figure 5.3 stall 12 appears to offer a better starting position in terms of profit. So how can a reliable draw bias be determined?

There are two methods that can be employed to determine the reliability of the stalls with regard to producing future profits. The first is based purely on the bettor's judgement whereas the second is based on a more rigorous statistical approach. The aim of the judgement based approach is to simply justify the profit/loss pattern produced by the analysis. In other words to find an adequate explanation for the results. The key factors to identify include whether the profitable stalls coincide with a perceived draw bias, for example on a round course are the profitable stalls located near to the inside running rail. A second important factor is whether the stalls adjacent to the profitable stall support the theory of a draw bias over mere chance. Thirdly, are the results produced by freak results, such as a $^{50}/_1$ winner? Once it has been established that the results are not a product of pure chance a betting rule, or system, can be formed.

The statistical approach concerns the calculation of a degree of confidence about the expected return for each stall. When a random sample is taken from a population, various statistical techniques can be applied to provide information about the reliability of the conclusions drawn from the sample. For example, it is possible to estimate the height of school leavers from a small sample of students. The average height of the students in the sample becomes an estimate of the average height of all students in the population from which the sample was drawn. However, the accuracy of this estimate is dependent on the size of the sample, and the distribution of the heights of students. Naturally, a very small sample, say one or two students, would provide no better information than an educated guess. And for populations which exhibit a high degree of variability, the estimation of the average value is clearly subject to a higher level of error than for a distribution which varies only slightly. By examining these factors it is possible to generate an estimate of the range of values the population average is likely to take. Consequently, by treating the results from each stall as a separate sample, it is possible to estimate, with a known degree of confidence, the likely level of profit/loss accounting for the number of races examined and the distribution of the starting prices of the winners.

To calculate this confidence interval it is necessary to derive the *standard deviation* of the sample. In other words to estimate the variability of the sample data. Once calculated a function of this value is used to derive the confidence interval. Figure 5.5 details the sample data for the Chester 5 furlong example previously discussed, for the horses running from stall 1.

Race Number	Starting Price	Finishing Position	Return (x)	Return^2 (x^2)
1	2/1	4	-1.00	1.00
2	2/1	4	-1.00	1.00
3	20/1	6	-1.00	1.00
4	11/2	7	-1.00	1.00
5	12/1	3	-1.00	1.00
6	7/2	1	3.50	12.25
7	9/4	4	-1.00	1.00
8	10/1	4	-1.00	1.00
9	9/1	1	9.00	81.00
10	11/1	3	-1.00	1.00
11	11/4	2	-1.00	1.00
12	8/1	6	-1.00	1.00
13	5/1	4	-1.00	1.00
14	50/1	5	-1.00	1.00
15	33/1	3	-1.00	1.00
16	10/1	2	-1.00	1.00
17	9/4	7	-1.00	1.00
18	14/1	1	14.00	196.00
19	7/2	2	-1.00	1.00
20	6/1	6	-1.00	1.00
21	8/1	2	-1.00	1.00
22	7/1	2	-1.00	1.00
23	9/2	4	-1.00	1.00
24	16/1	3	-1.00	1.00
25	7/2	1	3.50	12.25
26	20/1	6	-1.00	1.00
Total	-	-	8.00	323.50

Figure 5.5: Results from Chester 5 furlong handicap races

The return is calculated on a win basis for a level £1 stake, and in order to calculate the standard deviation of this variable it is necessary to first determine the squares of the values. These are presented in column five of figure 5.5. The variance of a distribution, σ^2, is given by the following equation, with the standard deviation simply the square root of the variance:

$$\sigma^2 = \frac{\sum_{i=1}^{n} x_i^2}{n} - \left(\frac{\sum_{i=1}^{n} x_i}{n}\right)^2$$

where x represents a sample value and n the sample size.

For the Chester example the variance becomes:

$$\sigma^2 = \frac{323.50}{26} - \left(\frac{8}{26}\right)^2$$

$$\therefore \sigma^2 = 12.35$$

Consequently, the standard deviation is $\sqrt{12.35}$ or 3.51.

The calculation of the confidence interval uses the standard deviation of the sample, the sample size, and a value taken from the t-distribution. (In fact, the calculation requires an estimate of the standard deviation of the population for which the standard deviation of the sample is a biased estimate and should therefore be adjusted. However, for reasonably large sample sizes this adjustment is minimal.) The equation for the confidence interval is given below:

$$\bar{x} \pm \frac{t\sigma}{\sqrt{n}}$$

where $\bar{x}$ is the average of the sample, t is a value from the t-distribution and σ is the standard deviation of the sample.

The t-value depends on the sample size and the degree of confidence required. Consequently, for a consistent sample size the t-value increases as the level of confidence increases. The most used confidence interval is 95%

which means that the average value of 95% of samples selected from the population would lie within the confidence interval. For large sample sizes the t-value for a 95% confidence interval approaches 1.96 and for samples of at least 20 it is quite close to 2.00. Therefore, using 2.00, for ease of calculation, is suggested.

For the Chester example, the confidence interval becomes:

$$CI = 0.308 \pm \frac{2 \times 3.51}{\sqrt{26}}$$

$$CI = 0.308 \pm 1.377$$

Therefore the 95% confidence interval for the average return (per £1 staked) ranges from -1.07 to 1.69. A lower limit of +0.1 would be considered a minimum to cover the betting tax. Although an average return of 30p per £1 staked may be considered a good rate of return, from the confidence interval it can be seen that the positive return may easily be due to chance alone. And the data support this conclusion, since removing the $^{14}/_1$ winner from the sample would have resulted in a loss of 24p per £1 staked. This highlights the value of the confidence interval. However, for betting purposes, where the element of *risk* is always present a lower degree of confidence may be considered acceptable which in some cases may result in a confidence interval that satisfies preset tolerance levels. For instance a 90% confidence interval with a t-value of just 1.7. This decision is left to the system developer.

There is one small reservation about this approach. In theory the sample needs to be selected from the whole population, however this is not possible for the horseracing problem since the whole population includes races in which we would like to bet. Therefore changing circumstances have not been accounted for, such as the moving of running rails or a change in the watering policy which could affect future results.

On some courses it is necessary to analyse the results by not only the race distance but the going and/or stall position. On tracks like Chester, the advantage of an inside draw is sometimes negated by a prolonged spell of wet weather since this part of the course becomes badly *cut up* by the continued pounding of the horses' hooves. Similarly, the position of the starting stalls can affect the outcome of the race. When the stalls were placed on the *inside* of the Southwell 5 furlong all weather course horses drawn low had a distinct advantage due to the shape of the course. However, for some years the stalls have always been placed on the outside for these sprint races nullifying the draw bias.

Notwithstanding these reservations, systems based on the draw are normally very reliable and can produce excellent returns. The following stalls have been found to offer excellent betting opportunities in previous seasons and, track modifications withstanding, should continue to provide a profitable return.

Course	Race Distance (f)	Draw
Epsom	8	1,2
Hamilton	5-6	H,H-1,H-2
Musselburgh	5	1,2
Sandown *(stalls far side)*	5	H,H-1
York	8-10	1,2

Figure 5.6: Profitable draw courses

In figure 5.6 *H* refers to the highest stall number, and *H-1* the next highest, and so on. Horses drawn in the highlighted stalls should be backed in non-juvenile handicap races on good or firmer ground except at Sandown where the ground restriction does not apply. In fact, the softer the ground at Sandown the greater the advantage to the high drawn horses.

References

[1] *Prediction Models in Horse Racing*, by Y. Dayan and D. L. McCartney, in *Proceedings of the Business and Economics Statistics Section*, American Statistical Association, pp508-512, 1981.

[2] *An Investigation of Decision Rules for Thoroughbred Race Horse Wagering*, by R. Vergin, *Interfaces*, Vol. 8, No. 1, pp34-45, 1977.

6

The Knowledge-Based Approach

The rule-based approach provides an easy to implement, and efficient solution to the horseracing problem. However, many rule-based systems ignore a vast amount of data which could possibly improve the selection method. In this chapter a more rigorous approach is discussed which utilises all relevant information.

Knowledge-Based Systems

The conceptual breakthrough made in the 1970's which led to the development of knowledge-based systems may be stated thus: to make a computer program intelligent provide it with lots of high-quality, specific knowledge about some problem area[1]. The main result of this innovation was *expert systems*.

Expert systems, the most common application of artificial intelligence, are knowledge-based systems, although the converse is not necessarily true. They employ the solution methods used by human experts in narrow well-defined domains to solve problems. Decision support systems, on the other hand, are again knowledge-based systems but do not always generate a solution. For example, a system designed to advise the operator with respect to the completion of a tax return is, in essence, supporting the user in the decision-making process and not making the decision itself, whereas a system designed to control the processes in a nuclear reactor may, in some instances, close down part or all of the device, effectively taking the action itself and not merely advising. For the horseracing problem the system is necessarily one of support since it will not be placing the actual bets merely recommending betting opportunities. However, the design and construction of the knowledge-based system proposed in this chapter is similar to the procedure followed for building an expert system.

There are two main components to an expert system: a knowledge base and an inference engine. As the name implies the knowledge base contains all the knowledge items the system developer has been able to distil from the experts and the available literature. This is where the power of an expert system lies, its detailed, in-depth, apparent *understanding* of a specific domain. As a rule, the knowledge-base is kept separate from the other parts of the system, i.e. from routines to handle the user interface, and it is written in a clear, readable fashion, which makes it more accessible to the operators and simplifies the process of adding new knowledge. Thus, the knowledge of an expert system can continue to be increased or modified after the official end of the development stage. This is not always the case with conventional computer programs. The inference engine controls the system and may be said to perform the reasoning. It adopts a suitable reasoning strategy, such as backward or forward chaining, to infer conclusions for the input query. The choice of inferencing procedure will depend upon the nature of the problem and the chosen mode of knowledge representation. In many cases though, a combination of techniques will be used.

An important decision in the development of an expert system is the selection of a format for representing the knowledge. There are several established formats, the most common of which are *rules*, *frames* and *semantic networks*. Rules are commonly used to represent diagnostic knowledge. As an example of a rule the following was taken from the MYCIN[2] system, one of the first working medical expert systems:

> *if   the gram stain of the organism is gramneg*
> *and   the morphology of the organism is rod*
> *and   the aerobicity of the organism is anaerobic*
> *then there is suggestive evidence (0.6) that the identity of the*
> *   organism is bacteroides*

The main use of rules is to represent the empirical associations between patterns of data and the actions that the system should perform as a consequence[3] or the conclusions it should reach. In addition, for a user familiar with the field, the above rule could form part of an explanation to help justify the output of the system. Frames, originated by Marvin Minsky, provide a means of representing the attributes of objects. A frame is in essence a data-structure for representing a stereotyped situation. Semantic networks are similar to frames and are associated with the representation of relationships between concepts. For the horseracing system discussed in this chapter, a rule-based representation was selected since it more closely mirrored the methods employed by expert race analysts. However, both frames and semantic networks could also be applicable to this problem.

As an example of how rules can be used to represent knowledge, and an inferencing strategy may work, consider the following simple rules which form part of a rule base used to evaluate the likely fitness of a horse.

Rule 1
if days since last run <= 42
then horse has run recently

Rule 2
if days since last run > 42
and days since last run <= 150
then horse has been unraced for a long time

Rule 3
if days since last run > 150
then horse has been unraced for a very long time

Rule 4
if horse has run recently
then horse is fit

Rule 5
if horse has been unraced for a long time
and horse runs well when fresh
then horse is fit

Rule 6

if   horse has been unraced for a long time
and   horse does not run well when fresh
then horse is not fit

Rule 7

if   horse has been unraced for a very long time
then horse is not fit

Set the query *is the horse fit?* the system may respond with the question: *has the horse run recently?* The user can answer *yes, no* or *don't know* to this question. The affirmative reply would *fire* rule 4 and the conclusion that the horse was fit would be derived. Answering *no* would probably send control to another part of the rule base. The *don't know* reply may result in the system asking how many days since the horse last run in an attempt to determine whether the horse had run recently or not. From this response the system would evaluate whether the horse has run recently or not and finally deduce the level of fitness.

Although these rules determine whether a horse is fit or not, the way they are presented in this example does not allow for uncertainty, nor the accumulation of evidence. In the following sections three different methods for handling uncertainty in a knowledge-base are discussed.

Dealing with Uncertainty in Rules

The ability to reason with inexact or uncertain data is a necessary skill most experts will possess and, as a consequence any computer system aimed at emulating the work of a human expert needs to reason in a similar way. Three common numerical approaches that can be used to provide a basis for reasoning under uncertainty, *Bayesian reasoning, fuzzy logic* and *certainty factors*, are discussed in this section.

Bayesian Reasoning

Bayes theorem, named after the English philosopher Thomas Bayes, concerns the calculation of conditional probabilities, and may be stated thus:

$$p(h|e) = \frac{p(h \cap e)}{p(e)}$$

where *h* is the hypothesis, *e* is the evidence and *p(x)* is the probability of *x*.

As an example, consider a patient exhibiting a symptom *s*, the examining physician will aim to diagnose the disease, *d*, from which the patient is suffering. In other words he/she will need to determine the conditional probability *p(d|s)* (i.e. the probability the patient has contracted disease *d* given that he/she has the symptom *s*). Bayes theorem breaks the problem down into two separate probabilities *p(d∩s)* and *p(s)*. However, in order to satisfy the equation *p(d∩s)* additional data in the form of prior probabilities are required: the doctor would need to know how many patients suffered from the disease, how many complained of the symptom, and how many, suffering from the disease, were also exhibiting the symptom. Clearly, such detailed prior probabilities are not always available particularly in less well defined domains and numerous approximations and assumptions would have to be incorporated into the calculation. The complexity of the problem is further increased if more than one symptom is displayed, especially if the symptoms are not conditionally independent of each other. A more detailed analysis of the shortcomings of Bayesian inference can be found in *Probability in Artificial Intelligence and Expert Systems* by Glenn Shafer[7].

Fuzzy logic

The theory of fuzzy logic is normally credited to the work of Lotfi A. Zadeh and his foundation paper entitled *Fuzzy Sets*[4]. However, it could be argued that fuzzy logic was initially founded by Gautama Buddha (c. 600 BC). Buddhism often refers to things in shades of grey as opposed to the more conventional two-valued, black-white logic. In fact the phrase "X is not-X" would be acceptable to most Buddhists (see Eberhart, Simpson and Dobbins[5] for a more detailed explanation).

Fuzziness refers to event ambiguity and provides a measure of the degree to which an event occurs, not whether it occurs[6]. In effect, fuzzy logic is an extension of classical set theory which is based on the concept that membership of a set is either true or false. For many real world situations this true-false distinction is far from satisfactory. Consider, for the purposes of illustration, the following example which is often quoted in this context:

Let the number of individual grains of corn contained within a large heap be defined as *many*. After removing only a single grain the heap would still be defined as containing *many* grains. Our definition would also hold after removing another grain. By induction, one could remove grains until only one remained and the definition would still hold.

Clearly, this is an absurd situation. The problem concerns the vagueness of the term *many* and its representation as a well defined set i.e. the number of grains is either *many* or *not many*. Fuzzy sets allow elements to be members to varying degrees, where *degree* is a real number between zero and one (inclusive). Consider this second example. A person standing 7 feet in height would be considered to be tall, and in contrast a person of only 4 feet would be considered short. To classify these people into two separate height sets would be possible using the following statements:

if height is 7 feet then tall is true and short is false
if height is 4 feet then short is true and tall is false

However, how would a person standing 5 feet 10 inches be categorised? In linguistic terms this person may be labelled quite tall. In fuzzy logic a height of 5 feet 10 inches could be represented as a membership of the two sets *tall* and *short*. For instance, membership of the set *tall* as 0.7 and membership of the set *short* as 0.1. Thus the absolute truth or falsehood of classical set theory is replaced by a continuous scale.

It can be shown that all the properties associated with classical set theory, such as commutativity and associativity, set union and intersection, are found within fuzzy set theory. For instance, given two fuzzy sets, f_1 and f_2, the operations of union and intersection may be defined as:

union $\quad : f_1$ or $f_2 \quad = \max(f_1, f_2)$
intersection $: f_1$ and $f_2 = \min(f_1, f_2)$

Therefore, the manipulation of fuzzy sets within a knowledge-based system does not present the computer programmer with a complex coding task.

The Bayesian approach to uncertain reasoning requires a detailed knowledge of prior probabilities, this is not the case for fuzzy logic. Furthermore, it has been suggested that fuzzy logic provides a simpler approach to reasoning with uncertainty than Bayesian logic consequently simplifying the form of the knowledge base. However, a major drawback concerns the accumulation of evidence. A reasoning process based on fuzzy logic does not take into account the quantity of available evidence to support the proposition, a feature which in some domains is not acceptable.

Certainty Factors

Certainty factors were developed to handle the uncertain reasoning in the MYCIN expert system[2]. The rules in MYCIN are presented in the following form:

if E_1 and E_2 and ... and E_n then $h(\alpha)$

where E_i is an item of evidence and α is the level of certainty relating to the conclusion h.

A simple method is used to combine two certainty factors, x and y, and is given below:

$$CF = \begin{cases} x + y - xy & \text{if } x, y \text{ are the same sign} \\ \dfrac{(x+y)}{\left[1 - \min(|x|,|y|)\right]} & \text{if } x, y \text{ are opposite signs} \end{cases}$$

where CF refers to the combined certainty factor and $|\cdot|$ is the modulus.

Certainty factors are incremental in their construction and account for the accumulation of evidence, consequently, it is easy to see how certainty factors could be used to evaluate many of the critical factors considered in Chapter 3. For instance, the rules which determine the suitability of the race conditions as well as fitness could be replaced with an iterative method based on certainty factors. As an example, the assessment of the going factor is based on rules of the following form:

> *if today's going is good*
> *and the horse has performed well on good going*
> *then today's going is suitable*

However, it would be possible for a horse to run well once on a particular state of ground and follow this by several poor runs on similar surfaces and be classified as being suited by that going. Adopting a certainty factor approach all previous races could be considered and a degree of confidence in the suitability of the going determined. Furthermore, this could be undertaken in just two rules.

> *if   going of historical race is the same as today's going*
> *and   horse performed well*
> *then   update going suitability assessment by 0.5*

> *if   going of historical race is similar to today's going*
> *and   horse performed well*
> *then   update going suitability assessment by 0.25*

In essence, the first rule states that, based on one race, it is only possible to be 50% sure that a horse is suited by any particular state of going. However, this percentage is not fixed and can easily be modified by the system developer. The second rule considers race performance on *similar* going to a particular state. In this case similar means differing by at most one going category, therefore, for good going for the forecast race both good to firm and good to soft would be considered to be *similar*. As a numerical example, consider a horse running on good to firm going which had previously run well on good to firm once, and had run well on firm (once) and good (twice). Using the percentages quoted in the above rules the assessment of going suitability is presented in figure 6.1.

Historical Performance Going	Increment Percentage	Cumulative Percentage
Good to firm	50%	50%
Firm	25%	62%
Good	25%	72%
Good	25%	79%

Figure 6.1: Going assessment using certainty factors

As the number of *good* race performances on the going (or a similar going) increases the suitability measure tends to 1 (i.e. complete confidence in the suitability of the going). For the example in figure 6.1 the final value is

79% indicating a high degree of confidence that the going is suitable which is not surprising given the historical race profile.

It is also possible to supplement the above rule base with negative certainty factors associated with poor race performance. Consider, for example, a horse which had run just twice, both times on the same ground performing well on its first run and poorly on its second. The rules quoted in Chapter 3 would indicate that the horse is suited by the surface, and the certainty factor approach quoted earlier would give the horse a 50% chance of being suited by the going. Adding the following two rules to the knowledge base, though, would change the assessment still further:

> *if going of historical race is the same as today's going*
> *and horse performed poorly*
> *then update going suitability assessment by -0.5*

> *if going of historical race is similar to today's going*
> *and horse performed poorly*
> *then update going suitability assessment by -0.25*

The assessment of going suitability based on the two contrasting race performances now becomes:

$$CF = \frac{0.5 - 0.5}{1 - 0.5} = 0$$

In other words from the available evidence it is not possible to say whether the horse is suited by the going or not which is a reasonable conclusion given that the horse has run twice on the going producing two completely different race performances. This approach accounts for all relevant information and is thus preferred, however, it does involve considerable more effort in calculating each of the critical factors and care needs to be taken when assigning the certainty factors for each rule.

Handling uncertainty in knowledge-bases is not an easy task, however, methods do exist that can be employed to good effect. For the horseracing problem, a Bayesian approach seems to provide the most appropriate solution. However, the requirement to calculate a range of conditional probabilities due to the dependence of a number of the variables and the sparseness of the data sets makes this technique difficult to implement. Fuzzy logic offers an attractive solution, especially when consideration is given to a requirement for explanation. For the horseracing problem, though, a mechanism which accounts for the accumulation of evidence is a prerequisite of any reasoning strategy, therefore, fuzzy logic does not provide an adequate solution method. Consequently, certainty factors are used for handling uncertainty in the knowledge-based systems developed in this chapter. In the next section it is demonstrated how certainty factors can be used, not to generate conclusions for individual factors, but to generate an overall assessment rating for each horse in the race.

Developing a Knowledge-Based System for Horseracing

The development of a knowledge-based, or expert, system can be considered as having five stages, illustrated in figure 6.2. The initial exercise is one of problem identification. The project aims need to be clearly stated and the key problem characteristics identified. This will always constitute the first stage of any system development project. Due to the nature and complexity of tasks addressed by knowledge-based systems, the knowledge acquisition phase, stage two, will overlap with the remaining three stages and will possibly be returned to after the testing phase. During this critical process the knowledge engineer (system developer) will attempt to extract, from a range of sources, the knowledge required by the system. It is generally accepted that the knowledge acquisition phase is one of the primary bottlenecks in the development of knowledge-based systems[1]. Whilst much of the knowledge required to build the system may be contained in available literature, the main source of input will often be human experts. The process of extracting this expert knowledge is normally very time consuming. Consequently, many researchers have devoted a great deal of time to this aspect of knowledge engineering and as a result a number of techniques have been established, the most popular being *structured interviews* and *protocol analyses*. Other techniques include *repertory grid analysis, rule induction by machine, case study observation* and *introspection*, details of which are beyond the scope of this text. Structured, or semi-structured, interviews are normally conducted in the early stages of the knowledge acquisition exercise and provide an effective method for obtaining an overview of the domain. One of the problems, however, is that the knowledge engineer is required to direct the process, which, given only limited understanding of the topic, is a difficult task. Protocol analysis offers a solution to this problem. The domain expert is asked to solve an existing problem and to comment aloud throughout the process. A transcript can be produced from a recording of the session which may then be analysed in detail. However, for the horseracing problem, races are evaluated each day in the Racing Post with detailed comments on each horse and a summary of the experts' conclusions. These can be used as case studies and a great deal of information regarding the solution methods employed by the race analysts obtained, reducing the need to interview several additional experts.

The decision on how best to represent the knowledge is dependent on the problem characteristics and will be greatly influenced by the knowledge already collected. In numerically based domains, this stage will also concern an element of data pre-processing the results of which may influence the choice of representational structure. Implementation of the system is the next step. A popular approach is *rapid prototyping*. This is an iterative process which involves repeatedly modifying and testing the system. New knowledge can be added and tested, with existing knowledge modified as a consequence or on the advice of experts in the domain. This process continues until the system satisfies the pre-set targets and can be considered complete.

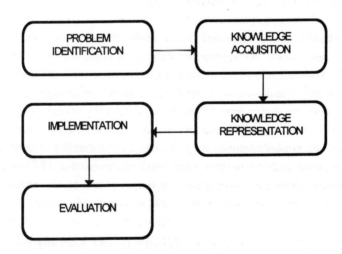

Figure 6.2: Stages in development of a knowledge-based system

There are two distinct parts to the horseracing problem. Firstly, it is necessary to generate assessments for each of the critical variables that constitute a horse profile. For instance, suitability of the going, likely level of fitness etc. The second stage involves combining these individual assessments into an overall evaluation of the horse which can be used to compare the runners in the race.

To generate a horse profile, the rules identified in Chapter 3 need to be coded into the knowledge-base. For instance, to determine the suitability of the going eight rules of the following form were coded:

> *if   today's going is good*
> *and   the horse has performed well on good going*
> *then today's going is suitable*

In total twelve factors are considered: ability, age, weight carried, assessments of the three most recent race performances, suitability of the going, suitability of the race distance, fitness, previous success rate, trainer's success rate and jockey's success rate. These factors are implemented as in Chapter 3 with a few minor modifications. The ability assessment is based on Raceform's Private Handicap rating, and is adjusted to account for biases in the draw and overweight carried by the jockey before rescaling to the highest value in the race (see figure 3.3).

Combining the twelve factors into a single rating can be achieved in many ways, but for this project the certainty factor approach was adopted. Each factor is associated with a chance of race success, such as 10.4% for horses which are considered to be race fit. These percentages can easily be combined using the certainty factor method. As an example, consider a horse racing in a non-juvenile race which is top rated (i.e. a rescaled rating of zero), and is suited by the race distance. The probability of success for top rated horses in non-juveniles races has been assessed at 17.7% (figure 3.3) and the success rate associated with horses suited by the race distance is 10.8%. Therefore, these two factors can be combined as follows:

$$CF = (0.177 + 0.108) - (0.177 \times 0.108)$$
$$CF = 0.266$$

The certainty factor of 26.6% could then be combined with another factor, such as suitability of the going, and so on until all the factors have been considered. Once this has been completed for each horse an order can be determined with the highest rated horse considered the most likely winner.

To test this approach 137 non-juvenile races were selected at random from the 1997 season. These races contained more than 1,100 runners at an average of just over 8 runners per race. An iterative modelling process was used, resulting in many different combinations of factors tested. Each model, though, contained the ability measure which was then supplemented with the other factors. Interestingly, three factors were found to be significant: the ability rating, the going suitability and the race distance suitability. Consequently, a very simple model resulted, with the other factors having a minimal effect on the model performance for these test races. Of course varying the methods for evaluating the profile components, or using different example races, may result in a more complex model.

For the 137 test races, the three factor model correctly assessed 52 races, with 80 of the 137 winners rated highest or second highest by the model. The success rate for highest rated horse at 38% (52 winners from 137 selections) compares to a random expectation of just over 15%, a significant improvement. Figure 6.3 presents the probability of success (i.e. ratio of winners to runners) against the model output.

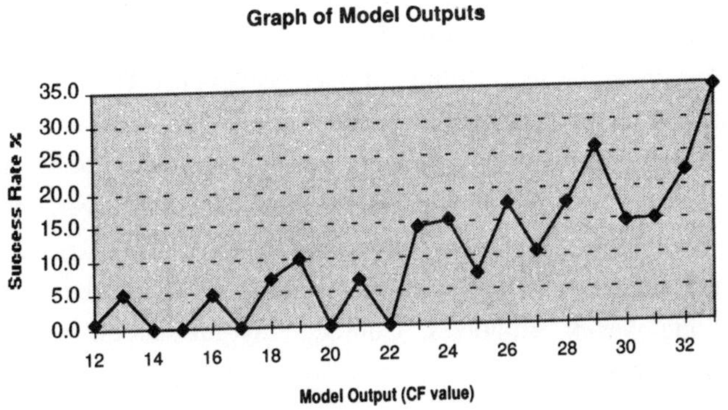

Graph of Model Outputs

Figure 6.3: Analysis of model performance

It can be seen that there exists a positive correlation between the model output and the success rate for all horses, which is to be hoped for in a model of this type.

The success rate for the highest rated horses of 38% combined with the strong positive correlation between success rate and model output suggests that the model possesses a reasonable degree of forecasting ability. However, for the horseracing problem the most important information from an evaluation is the profit/loss data. For the 137 races the highest rated horse returned a profit of 30p per £1 staked. And a 95% confidence for the sample placed the population mean between 0.11 and 0.49, implying a profit, after tax, at starting price even for the lower bound of the interval.

Interestingly, of the 137 selected horses (i.e. those highest rated by the model) not all were considered suited by the going or race distance. In fact, 18 selections were not proven on the ground (9 winners and 9 losers) and 17 were classified as being unproven over the race distance. However, as expected the 137 selections do possess a bias with respect to the ability rating. More than half of the selections, 87 in fact, were assigned the highest ability rating. Of these 36 were successful, a strike rate of just over 41%. From the remaining 50 selections, 41 were attributed an ability rating of within 10lbs of the highest rated horse, with the lowest rated animal some 31lbs adrift.

In Chapter 4 a method was discussed for fitting a logistic curve to the model output to provide an estimate of the probability of success, thus accounting for the within race competition. Applying this technique to the output from the model facilitates a second analysis of the data which restricts the selections to just those horses for which the starting price is greater than the forecast *fair* price. Of the 137 highest rated horses only 41 satisfied the price constraint (i.e. the starting price was equal or greater than the calculated fair price). Of these 41 selections, 11 won, a strike rate of just 26.8% some way below the strike rate for all highest rated horses. However, the average return per £1 staked increased from 30p to 85p. These results are not unexpected, since this technique shifts the emphasis from predicting winners to identifying over-priced horses. Consequently, the success rate in terms of winners decreases.

The knowledge-base which forms the basis of the forecasting model detailed in this section is of a very simplistic form. The knowledge itself is quite shallow with rules consisting of a relatively low number of antecedents. However, the system could easily be extended to include knowledge of greater depth. The main area for improvement is the derivation of the individual conclusions for the horse profile. An approach which uses the certainty factors to generate several of these intermediate conclusions has already been discussed. This has the benefit of using all of the available information and uses both positive and negative evidence to generate the conclusions. However, the critical assessment is that of a race performance since it has a bearing on several of the intermediate conclusions. The current approach uses a set of rules to classify a race performance into three categories: *good, moderate* or *poor*. Whilst this appears to perform to a satisfactory standard, race performance is a fuzzy concept, likewise the classifications, and ideally should be treated as such. Due to the form of the classification, not all race performances will be clustered in the centre of one of the three categories, some will be very borderline cases. This is always the case when attempting to classify a continuous measure into discrete classes. An approach which classifies race performance as membership of performance sets may produce better results. This would be similar to the height example discussed in the fuzzy logic section of this chapter. Representing race performances in this way would require many more certainty factors to be calculated (just three are required for the current method). However, given the availability of historical data this should not present a significant problem.

A second area which could be extended is the use of ratings for the ability measure. Not all horses are rated: some horses trained abroad will not have been rated and, naturally, a horse making its debuts will not have a rating. In these cases the forecast starting prices can be used to estimate the rating since quite a strong correlation exists between these two variables. A slightly more complex problem is posed by horses which have raced on only a few occasions. The ratings for these animals are less reliable than for the more exposed horses and subject to significant change after each race. For these runners, a more accurate reflection of their ability can be gained from combining the rating with the trainer's success rate with similar animals. For example, the rules could take the following form:

> *if   horse has raced less than n times*
> *then ability = f(rating, trainer's strike rate, number of previous runs)*

In the example rule a threshold number of races could be set at, say, 4. The ability rating then becomes a function of the current rating, the trainer's success rate and the number of times the horse has run for animals which have raced fewer than five times. This function could take one of several forms, such as a multiple regression model, or another rule base.

The knowledge-based approach discussed in this chapter offers a very satisfactory solution to the horseracing problem in several respects. It has been demonstrated that even a simple knowledge-base can produce good test results, and it is distinctly possible that a more sophisticated model would produce better results. Knowledge-bases are relatively easy to construct, although a great deal of data analysis is required, but more importantly they are easy to modify or supplement with new information, for instance at the end of each season.

Reference Classes

The reference class approach offers an alternative method for comparing the profiles of the runners. As in the previous section, the knowledge-base(s) are used to evaluate each component of the animal's profile, the comparison is then made by matching this profile to historical records for which the race results are known. A ratio of historical winners to runners is recorded for the matched pairs which can then be transformed into odds by a simple normalising procedure.

As an example, consider a horse profile which consists of just two components: ability rating and going suitability. The first step in this procedure is to divide each component into sub-categories. For this example, the ability rating is divided into two categories: *top rated* and *other*; the going suitability factor is divided into three categories: *suitable*, *unsuitable* and *unknown*. Therefore, a horse is classified into one of six classes illustrated in figure 6.4.

Ability Rating	Going Suitability	Class No.
Top Rated	Suitable	1
Top Rated	Unknown	2
Top Rated	Not Suitable	3
Not Top Rated	Suitable	4
Not Top Rated	Unknown	5
Not Top Rated	Not Suitable	6

Figure 6.4: Possible reference classes

This categorisation needs to be performed for all historical records as well as for the horses under consideration. Once completed the new horse profiles can be compared to each historical record and the ratio of winners to losers determined. It is at this stage that a minor problem can arise. For detailed horse profiles with many sub-categories, a great deal of historical data is required to provide a reasonable number of matches. For instance, eight factors in the profile each divided into three sub-categories generates over 6,500 (i.e. 3^8) possible classes. Consequently, a vast amount a historical data would be required. There are several ways to solve this problem. The obvious solution is to use more historical data, however, as discussed in Chapter 5, very old data may not remain relevant today so care needs to be taken with this approach. A second solution involves the reclassification of the factors, by making some of the sub-categories larger (those into which few historical records are grouped) or by reducing the total number of sub-categories. The third method is to process the record and check the number of matches. If this is found to be insufficient, one of the factors (the least important) is dropped and the matching process is repeated for the reduced profile. This continues until a satisfactory number of matches is found. However, this final approach does depend on the system developer identifying the least important classes.

Reference Classes: Example

In this example the reference class approach is applied to juvenile non-handicap races. As with any forecasting problem selecting the variables for inclusion in the model and representing the data are critical stages of development. This is of particular importance to reference class applications since too many, or poorly categorised, factors will result in a poor distribution of historical cases and hence a far from uniform distribution of matched cases. A major problem when designing forecasting methods for juvenile races, though, is the lack of information. Many juveniles will not have raced before and as a consequence will not have the all important ability rating. Furthermore, unless the pedigree is examined in detail, the suitability of the race conditions will also be unknown for these runners. Therefore, for this example, it was considered appropriate to create two different profiles, one for unraced horses and a second for horses which have raced.

For unraced horses the profile consists of three components: the rating of the highest rated horse in the race, the trainer's success rate with juvenile debutants and the month. Each of these components is divided into the following sub-categories:

Component	Cat. 1	Cat. 2	Cat. 3	Cat. 4	Cat. 5
Max. Rating	100+	80-99	60-79	1-59	no rating

Component	Cat. 1	Cat. 2	Cat. 3
Trainer's Strike Rate	25%+	10%-24.9%	0%-9.9%

Component	Category 1	Category 2
Month	March-May	June-November

The trainer's strike rate for debutants is the only factor directly related to the horse and is an obvious variable for inclusion since it provides a measure of likely success for this type of horse. Some trainers seem more able to get their horses to (near) peak fitness for their first outing, an important consideration when evaluating juvenile races. The maximum race rating provides a guide to the standard of race in which the horse is entered, and indicates the level of ability the newcomer will need to possess in order to beat the previously raced animals. The month indicator isolates the early part of the season. The better juveniles tend to make their debuts later in the year so an average juvenile will have a better chance of success in the early months compared to the summer and autumn races.

For horses which have previously raced a more detailed profile is available, and seven factors are considered: adjusted speed rating, going suitability, distance suitability, number of previous runs, trainer's strike rate, number of days since last run and the month. Both the month and trainer's strike rate are sub-divided as for unraced horses, the other factors are divided as follows:

Component	Cat. 1	Cat. 2	Cat. 3	Cat. 4	Cat. 5
Adj. Rating	0	1-5	6-10	11-20	21+

The method used to generate the adjusted rating is the same as that given in Chapter 3 where each rating is subtracted from the highest race rating.

Component	Cat. 1	Cat. 2	Cat. 3
Going Suitability	Suitable	Unknown	Unsuitable

In Chapter 3 the going factor was sub-divided into two categories: suitable and unsuitable. For this application though a third, *unknown*, category has been added. This category merely isolates the horses which have not encountered the prevailing going from the remainder.

Component	Category 1	Category 2
Distance Suitability	Proven Form	No Proven Form

Component	Category 1	Category 2
No. of Previous Runs	1-2	3+

Component	Category 1	Category 2
Days since last run	1-40	41+

Clearly, the division of the factors is a decision for the model developer depending on previously gained knowledge. Although this representation is used in this particular example, many other representations exist and several will no doubt provide better results.

For testing purposes, 103 races comprising almost 1,000 horses were sampled. A further 7,500 different example race performances constituted the historical set. Using these reference classes the lowest number of matches between the horses in the test set and the historical records was 16, which was thought acceptable. Therefore no other modifications were required. The ratios generated by this approach ranged from zero (i.e. no winners in the matched historical examples) to 0.6, before normalisation. These results are presented graphically in figure 6.6.

The normalisation process is simply a matter of ensuring that the sum of the ratios for all horses in the race equals 1. This is achieved by calculating the aggregate of the ratios and then dividing each in turn by this figure. After normalisation the probabilities can easily be converted to odds, an analysis of which is presented in figure 6.7. A problem can arise, though, when the ratio for a horse is zero. For this case the odds cannot be calculated (due to division by zero) and therefore an arbitrary price is used, for instance 33/1 or

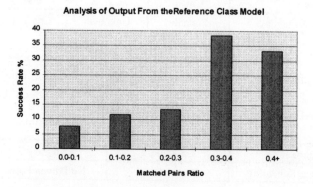

Figure 6.6: Analysis of model output for juvenile races

some other high price. Normalising the outputs accounts for the within race competition and generates a new distribution of probabilities. These can be directly compared to the odds offered by the bookmakers to determine whether a value betting option exists.

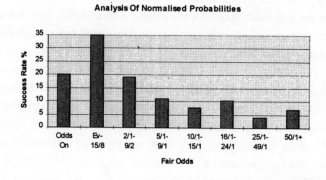

Figure 6.7: Analysis of normalised probabilities

For the reference class approach a selection is determined by the winners to runners ratio for the matched cases. The horse with the highest ratio is deemed to be the most likely winner and hence becomes the selection. Of the 103 selected horses, 28 were successful, a success rate of about 27%. This compares to a random expectation of just 12.8% for the same races. The average return for the selections was 52p per £1 staked, significantly higher than the 9p required for returning a profit after tax. Of the selections, 15 (4 winners, 87p profit per £1 staked) had a speed rating of more than 20 pounds inferior to the highest rated horse, illustrating that this method can identify winners which, on form, have little chance of success.

These results are very encouraging and show that the reference class method can be used to good effect in forecasting models for horseracing. The approach is easy to implement and maintain, although a large historical file can take some time to search. Updating the method is simply a matter of adding new records to the historical file as they become available, however as this file increases in size the opportunity should be taken to refine the classes and hopefully improve the success rate.

Summary

The advantages with knowledge-based systems include the simplicity of construction and modification. Unlike intensive numerical methods, it is easy to *see* what is happening in a knowledge-base and as a result justify the output. Consequently, modifications are easily made and potential weaknesses identified. Furthermore, these systems require no advanced programming skills and could be built using a spreadsheet. In this chapter two different applications of knowledge-based systems have been discussed, and two simple systems developed. More complex knowledge-bases comprising hundreds of rules are straightforward to construct using the principles identified in this section providing that adequate data (or domain knowledge) is available, and it is quite possible that such systems would produce better results.

References

[1] *A Guide to Expert Systems,* by D. A. Waterman, published by Addison-Wesley, Reading, MASS., USA, 1986.

[2] *Rule-Based Expert Systems,* by B. G. Buchanan and E. H. Shortliffe, published by Addison-Wesley, Reading, MASS., USA, 1984.

[3] *Introduction to Expert Systems,* by P. Jackson, published by Addison-Wesley, Wokingham, England, 1990.

[4] *Fuzzy Sets,* by L. A. Zadeh, in Information and Control, Vol. 8, pp338-353, 1965.

[5] *Computational Intelligence PC Tools,* by R. C. Eberhart, P. K. Simpson and R. C. Dobbins, published by Academic Press Limited, London, 1996.

[6] *Neural Networks and Fuzzy Systems: A Dynamical Systems Approach to Machine Intelligence,* by B. Kosko, published by Prentice Hall International, Englewood Cliffs, N. J., USA, 1992.

[7] *Probability Judgement in Artificial Intelligence and Expert Systems,* by G. Shafer, in Statistical Sciences, Vol. 2, 1987.

7

The Neural Network Approach

The success of knowledge-based and expert systems relies on the restricted and specialised nature of the domains to which they are applied. Such domains are usually well structured and do not rely on intuition based decision-making. For instance, technical expertise can be captured in an expert system, and some game playing problems and puzzle solving tasks where the knowledge required by the system can be easily expressed in rule form, are also applicable. However, many types of decision-making tasks cannot be solved by the symbolic approach of knowledge-based systems. For instance, these systems are not appropriate for tasks which are poorly defined and hence cannot be solved with an algorithmic approach, or for problems which contain a large volume of noisy data. These tasks are better approached from a connectionist perspective with the knowledge learned directly from example cases by the system itself and without the constraints of representing the knowledge in easily accessed symbolic structures. In this chapter the applicability of connectionist systems is examined with regard to the horseracing problem.

Artificial Neural Networks

What better model for a powerful computing machine is there than the human brain? As researchers have become more aware of the structure and processing methods of the brain the temptation to replicate it on a machine has become overwhelming. Artificial neural networks have been inspired by the limited knowledge gained from these biological advances.

Like the brain, artificial neural networks consist of many connected *neurons* (nodes), although the number differs significantly between the two mechanisms. It has been suggested[1] that the human brain has approximately 10^{11} active nodes on average, whereas the number in its artificial equivalent will rarely exceed a few thousand. The biological neurons receive many signals which are modified by a biochemical weight at the receiving synapse. These weighted inputs are combined by the soma (or body cell) and under appropriate circumstances the neuron transmits a signal. The mechanics of artificial nodes are modelled on these processes, where incoming signals are adjusted by weights, are summed, and, dependent on the activation function, a strong or weak signal is passed to the connecting nodes. Although similarities exist between biological and artificial neural networks, they differ in both function and form, especially how the nodes are connected and pass signals. The artificial network is, as one would expect, very much a simplification of the biological network.

Essentially, neural networks learn by example. They need no formal programming nor any initial coding of *knowledge* relating to the problem under consideration[†] . Instead, the network formulates its own knowledge from the examples it encounters during a period of training. Although this approach may seem somewhat *ad hoc*, it has been shown that neural networks can identify relationships between the data which had previously been overlooked by experienced domain experts, and in fact, it has been proved that given a sufficient number of hidden nodes, a neural network can be trained to perform any mapping operation. It is, therefore, easy to see the appeal of these networks given their simplicity of construction and classification power.

Brief Sketch of the History of Connectionist Systems

The first published work relating to the structure and function of the human brain is attributed to the American psychologist William James[2]. In his *Elementary Principle*, published in 1890, James discussed some of the basic concepts relating to correlational learning and associative memory referring to brain processes influencing each other. He also alluded to the concept of

---

† Some neural networks are structured to represent domain knowledge, such as knowledge-based neural networks.

a neuron's activity being related to the sum of its inputs.

Using these ideas, McCulloch and Pitts[3] developed in 1943 what is generally regarded as the first neural network. They combined many simple neurons into a neural system. The neurons can be arranged to produce any output that can be represented as a combination of logic functions. By the end of the decade, Donald Hebb[4] proposed a learning law which explained how a network of neurons learned, and in 1958 Rosenblatt[5] developed the perceptron learning algorithm.

In 1960, Widrow and Hoff[6] introduced an algorithm which dramatically reduced the time required for the perceptrons to classify patterns, and improved its accuracy. The Widrow-Hoff algorithm is a form of supervised learning which adjust weights in relation to the size of the error on the output.

Although the publication of the book *Perceptrons*[7] by Marvin Minsky and Seymour Papert, which illustrated the theoretical limitations of single-layer models, engendered a negative atmosphere in the neural network research community, work still continued and in 1986 Rumelhart, Hinton and Williams[8] offered a powerful solution to the training problems of multilayer neural networks, namely the back-propagation algorithm. It should be noted, though, that the idea of back-propagation had also been developed independently by Werbos[9] in 1974 and Parker[10] in 1982. Since the mid-eighties, there has been a dramatic increase in the number of variations of neural computing techniques due to the increased interest in the field and the increasing power of available computers. And nowadays the technology is becoming common-place in many environments outside the realms of the science laboratory.

Neural Network Learning

Neural network learning can be divided into two distinct areas: unsupervised learning and supervised learning. The essential difference between these two approaches is the use of the correct classification for each training pattern in the supervised learning method. Unsupervised learning, also referred to as self-organisation, is essentially data clustering. A feature of this approach is that unsupervised methods need to determine the pattern-class information as part of the learning process. Two examples of this type of learning are

Hebbian learning and Kohonen learning[11]. Pattern recognition is one area in which this type of network excels, with systems designed which can differentiate between hand-written characters, or signatures. The reference class approach described in Chapter 6 would be classified as unsupervised learning since the historical cases are clustered based on their features without reference to the race result (the target classification). In contrast, supervised learning classifies the input patterns depending on the pattern classes associated with each pattern. For each training pattern the correct response, or target value, is included with the input parameters. This target value represents the correct classification of the pattern. The most common supervised learning algorithm is the back-propagation of errors learning rule, or more simply back-propagation[9,8]. Briefly, back-propagation uses the *gradient descent* optimisation technique. The aim of gradient descent is to minimise the error between the calculated output (i.e. function approximation) and the actual output. Considering this difference as a function, the algorithm needs to find its lowest value (or global minimum). Gradient descent examines the gradient of this function to determine the direction in which it is most rapidly decreasing; this provides the necessary information for the weight updating procedure. In practice, a pattern is passed through the network and the difference between the network's calculated output and the correct output (i.e. the target output) is determined. The network's weights are then adjusted (i.e. the error is propagated back through the network), with the amount of weight adjustment controlled by the *learning rate*, a parameter which can take any value in the [0,1] range and is set by the network developer. A more detailed algorithm for the back-propagation process which can easily be incorporated into a computer program is given in appendix A3. However, many neural network back-propagation simulators are available as shareware on the internet in addition to the freeware simulator which accompanies this book (*see* appendix A4).

The Topology of Feedforward Neural Networks

Artificial neural networks are generally arranged in layers. Each layer consists of a number of nodes which are linked to the next layer either completely or partially. Nodes can take one of three forms: input, hidden or output. Input nodes are activated when an input pattern is presented to the network. The activation of each of these nodes is then combined with the weights of its connections and the output either excites or inhibits the connected hidden nodes. It is the activation of the hidden nodes (the final hidden layer if the architecture of the network comprises more than one) which influences, in conjunction with the weights, the activation of the output nodes. An example of a fully connected network, with one hidden layer, is given in figure 7.1. This network is known as a *multilayer perceptron* and is the chosen network for the horseracing application. In some network architectures, such as *Recurrent Networks*, the links can connect nodes to the previous layer as well as to the next layer, however in feedforward networks (as in figure 7.1) the connections are restricted to a single direction (from the input layer, via the hidden layer to the output layer).

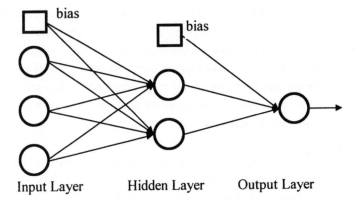

Input Layer   Hidden Layer   Output Layer

Figure 7.1: A fully connected multilayer perceptron

The network illustrated in figure 7.1 has one hidden layer consisting of two nodes. Whilst it is most common to have one hidden layer in a network, networks can be developed with any number of these layers.

Although there appears to be four nodes in the input layer, the square node is merely a bias (a node with its value always set to one). Including a bias is equivalent to incorporating a constant into the network function. There is also a bias acting on the output node. Consequently, this network would be referred to as a 3-2-1 network (i.e. three input nodes, two hidden nodes and one output node). This type of feedforward neural network, trained by back-propagation, is the chosen architecture for the horseracing problem.

The degree to which a hidden or output node is active depends on the activation of the nodes connected to it, the weights of the connections from these nodes and the *activation function*. For the ith hidden node the relationship is given in equation 7.1.

$$a_i(\mathbf{x}) = f\left(w_{i0} + \sum_{j=1}^{n} x_j \cdot w_{ij} \right) \qquad (7.1)$$

where w_{ij} represents the weight of the connection from the jth input node, w_{i0} is the weight from the input layer bias, x_j is the activation of the jth input node, and f is the activation function.

Hence, it can be seen that in the 3-2-1 network given in figure 7.1, the output is determined by the product of the weights connecting it to the hidden nodes and the activation of the hidden nodes themselves, plus the weight from the bias. However, the hidden nodes are, in turn, determined by the product of the weights from the three input nodes, the input node values and the bias. Although all the calculations are performed sequentially, the architecture of the system is essentially parallel.

Activation functions are also referred to as threshold functions or squashing functions. Although the possible number of activation functions is infinite, there are five families of functions which are normally used in the majority of networks[12]: i) linear; ii) step; iii) ramp; iv) sigmoid and v) Gaussian. Of these, the sigmoid function (equation 7.2) is the most popular due to its form (i.e. it is differentiable everywhere and is monotonically increasing).

$$f(x) = \frac{1}{1 + e^{-\alpha x}} \qquad (7.2)$$

α is a constant.

Normally, α is set to one (and is assumed to be one in all networks referred to in this book unless otherwise stated), however adjusting this constant will affect the slope of the function (figure 7.2). The effect of the sigmoid activation function is to constrain the activation of each node to the [0,1] range and introduce non-linearity into the network.

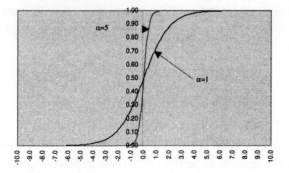

Figure 7.2: Sigmoid functions with α=1 and α=5

As an example of node activation consider the following weights connecting two input nodes and a bias to a hidden layer node.

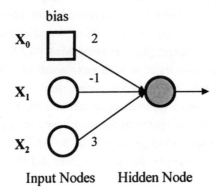

Figure 7.3: Activation of a hidden node

Setting the values of the two input nodes, x_1 and x_2, both to one, and using the sigmoid activation function with α set to 1, the activation of the hidden node becomes:

$$h_{act} = \frac{1}{1+e^{-(2-1+3)}} = \frac{1}{1+e^{-4}} = 0.98$$

This value would then be scaled by the weights which connect it to another layer of nodes i.e. an output node. Changing the values of the inputs will change the level of activation of this hidden node. For instance, setting the input node values both to zero results in an activation of 0.88 calculated from just the bias:

$$h_{act} = \frac{1}{1 + e^{-2}} = 0.88 \,.$$

In essence, neural networks are networks of very simple processing units which combine together to perform the mappings of the input patterns to the outputs.

Neural Network Development

There are four distinct steps in developing a neural network: data processing, design of the network architecture, network training/testing and finally validation. Data processing may involve feature extraction and other pre-processing techniques previously discussed, before conversion of the data into a form acceptable to the network. Most neural networks use normalised data i.e. data in the range [0,1] or sometimes [-1,1]. Consequently, the minimum and maximum value of each input needs to be determined prior to normalising the data. The normalisation itself is simply a matter of subtracting the minimum value an input can take for the data item and then dividing by the difference between the minimum and maximum values. For example, the age input can range from 2 to 15. An input pattern with an age parameter of 10, for example, can be normalised as follows:

$$N(age) = \frac{age - \min(age)}{\max(age) - \min(age)}$$

$$\therefore N(10) = \frac{10 - 2}{15 - 2} = 0.615$$

The performance of a neural network can be very sensitive to the way the data are represented. Consequently, great care needs to be taken with this aspect of network development. Representing categorical, or discrete feature data is relatively straightforward with an input node assigned to each category. For instance, to distinguish between non-handicap and handicap races in the network, two input nodes would be required, the first could be set to 1 for non-handicaps (with the other zero) and the reverse pattern used for handicap races. Real-valued inputs on a continuous scale can also be represented by single units with the complete input range mapped to the [0,1] range of the unit. Whilst discrete data, such as a scale from 1 to 10, can be represented in the same way, other representations may improve the network's performance. For instance, a binary representation. Naturally, this requires several input nodes to represent the variable but may result in reduced training times. However, it should be realised that with this approach two similar input values have totally different network representations. An alternative approach is to use a type of *thermometer* coding. As an example, consider the ages of horses. Although continuous, these values are presented in discrete form, such as 2, 3, 4, and so on. A thermometer code representation of the ages from 2 to 10 would require 9 inputs. For a two-year-old horse the first node would be set to one with the remainder set to zero. For a three-year-old, the first and second nodes would be set to one, and for a four-year-old the first three units would be set to one, with the remainder left at zero. In figure 7.4 the age of a seven-year-old horse is represented in the thermometer coding style.

Node	1	2	3	4	5	6	7	8	9
Value	1	1	1	1	1	1	0	0	0

Figure 7.4: Data representation

After the data processing and normalising stage the architecture of the network can be determined. The number of input nodes is simply the number required to represent the data in the chosen format. However, deciding on the number of hidden nodes is not so straightforward. The required size of the hidden layer is dependent on the complexity of the mapping the neural network is attempting to approximate. However, this is unknown prior to training, and hence the required number of hidden nodes is also unknown. As a guide though, the maximum number of hidden nodes should not exceed twice the number of input nodes, and the minimum number is zero since it is not always necessary to have a hidden layer. Various start points have been suggested such as half (or three-quarters) of the number of input nodes, but it should be remembered that the more hidden nodes used the more time each training cycle will take because there are more weights to update each pass. Consequently, it is possibly best to start with the fewest number considered necessary (zero maybe?) and then to increase the number if the network fails to find an acceptable mapping.

Once the architecture of the network has been decided, the network can begin training. The aim of the training phase is to adjust the internal weights of the network so that relationships are determined between the input patterns and the associated outputs. During training each pattern in the training set will be presented in turn to the network and the difference between the calculated output and the target output deduced. This difference is then used to modified the weights. A *cycle* (or *epoch*) is completed when all the patterns in the training set have been presented. Neural network training will often involve many training cycles (sometimes thousands, see the following example) which can make the process very time consuming. After each cycle an error term is updated to provide a means of determining how well the network is converging to a minimum, or how well the network mapping is classifying the patterns. This normally takes the form of the mean squared error which is simply the average of the squared differences between the calculated output and target output for each training pattern. As training progresses and the network mapping function improves, this value will gradually decrease. Alternatively, a measure of the system's progress can be determined by using a *test* set of patterns. The test set contains patterns which differ from those in the training set and is used to determine how well the network generalises to previously unseen examples. Once the network performs to a satisfactory degree on the test set, or the mean squared error has reached a sufficiently low level, the network can be validated on a third, distinct, set of examples.

Neural Network Development: Example

This example uses one of the most popular learning problems in the neural networks field: the exclusive OR problem. The exclusive OR, or XOR, data set contains only four patterns, presented in figure 7.5. The aim of a neural network trained on this data set is to discriminate between the two classes of output vector, and associate the input pairs with the value of zero, when $x_1 = x_2$ and one when $x_1 \neq x_2$. The network architecture for this problem consists of two input nodes, two hidden nodes and one output node (2-2-1). A sigmoid activation is used together with the back-propagation learning algorithm, and a learning rate set at 0.1.

Input x_1	Input x_2	Target Output
1	1	0
0	1	1
1	0	1
0	0	0

Figure 7.5: The XOR data set

Network training starts with weight initialisation. This process randomly assigns a set of weights to the network. It is normal practice to use a randomisation method which generates low weights (i.e. [-1, 1]) since large weights can saturate the hidden nodes producing hidden node values of close to 1 for any input pattern. Consequently, this can seriously inhibit the training process. For this problem the initial weights are given in figure 7.6.

From Input:	To Hidden Node h_1	To Hidden Node h_2	From Hidden:	To Output Node
node x_1	+0.85	+0.09	node h_1	-0.14
node x_2	-0.50	-0.99	node h_2	+0.21
bias	-0.29	-0.37	bias	-0.50

Figure 7.6: Initial weights for XOR network

It is possible to calculate the mean squared error for the network before training starts by checking how well the random weights classify the patterns. This analysis is given in figure 7.7, where the total squared error is given as 1.0597. Therefore the mean squared error is 0.265 (i.e. 1.0597/4).

X_1	X_2	Target Output	Network Output	Difference^2
1	1	0	0.3715	0.1380
0	1	1	0.3774	0.3876
1	0	1	0.3779	0.3870
0	0	0	0.3836	0.1471
			Total:	**1.0597**

Figure 7.7: Network performance before training

After 4,500 training cycles the network error has reduced to 0.05 at which point training is terminated. The reduction in the mean squared error is shown graphically in figure 7.8. It can be seen that many cycles are required before the network begins to converge, however after 2,500 cycles the error reduces rapidly, and a low level of error is soon achieved.

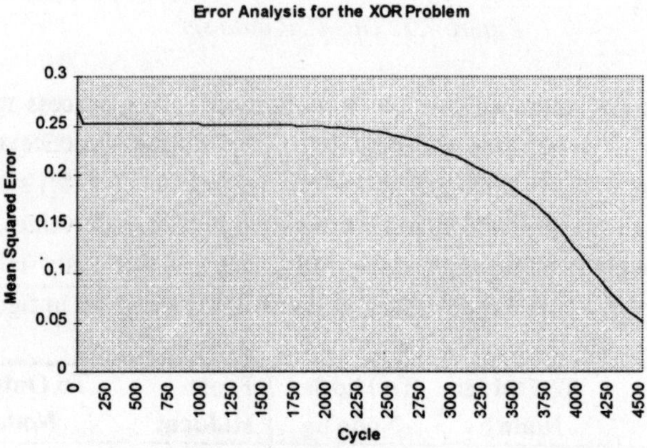

Error Analysis for the XOR Problem

Figure 7.8: Mean squared error by training cycle

When training is complete the weights have changed significantly, which can be seen from figure 7.9. These changes are due to the training process and represent the *knowledge* learned by the network from the examples. It is interesting to note the degree of symmetry about the weights which is in agreement with the symmetrical form of the training patterns and network architecture.

From Input:	To Hidden Node h_1	To Hidden Node h_2	From Hidden:	To Output Node
node x_1	3.40	4.40	node h_1	-4.17
node x_2	-3.07	-4.50	node h_2	4.98
bias	1.37	-2.77	bias	1.68

Figure 7.9: Weights for trained XOR network

For the XOR problem the entire data set is used to train the network. This is unusual, in real world applications only a part of the data set is used for training with the remainder used for testing and network validation. Consequently, testing the network with the training patterns is of limited value, however, it does show the capabilities of the network. Furthermore, it is possible to supplement these *test* vectors with other patterns which comprise real numbers and differ from the initial training set. Figure 7.10 presents the test vectors and the associated network output.

Input x_1	Input x_2	Known Output	Network Output
1	1	0	0.17
0	1	1	0.74
1	0	1	0.85
0	0	0	0.21
0.50	0.50	-	0.19
0.95	0.05	-	0.80
0.05	0.95	-	0.70

Figure 7.10: Network performance before training

From figure 7.10 it can be seen that, if presented with the pattern (1,1) the network would respond with a value close to zero (i.e. 0.17). An input pattern of (1,0) produces an output of 0.85; and the pattern (0.95,0.05) returns a value of 0.8. For this last pattern there is no correct response, however, given its closeness to the (1,0) input pattern an almost equal response seems to be a reasonable output. Although this is a very simplistic example, it is easy to see how these training patterns, on a larger scale, could represent the profiles of horses and the target values the race results with the network generating the necessary knowledge to produce reliable forecasts for future races.

As a second example, consider the data presented in figure 7.11. Essentially, the network needs to determine a mapping for one input such that when the input is 0, 0.5 or 1 the output is near zero, and for input values of approximately 0.25 and 0.75 the output should be near one.

A 1-12-1 feedforward network was trained on these data patterns, using a learning rate of 0.1, the back-propagation algorithm and sigmoid activation function. Training was halted at 1,000, 2,000 and 5,000 cycles and the network performance checked against a second data set. The results of these tests are given in figure 7.12.

Input x_1	Target Output
0.00	0
0.05	0
0.20	1
0.25	1
0.30	1
0.45	0
0.50	0
0.55	0
0.70	1
0.75	1
0.80	1
0.95	0
1.00	0

Figure 7.11: Training data for one input network

Clearly, as the number of cycles increases the closer the mapping gets to the training data. After just 1,000 cycles the output approximates a quadratic, whereas for 2,000 and 5,000 cycles the mapping is clearly more complex.

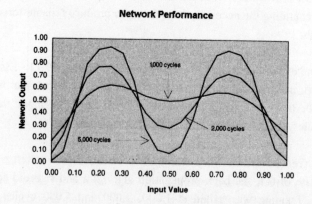

Figure 7.12: Test output from the three networks

This demonstrates how the network can be used to approximate complex non-linear mapping functions.

Although the four training patterns of the XOR example are relatively learned easily by the network, there can be problems with the training phase. The aim of gradient descent methods (used in back-propagation) is to locate the *global minimum* of the error function, this is the point where the function most closely matches the training patterns. However, there are cases where a *local minimum* is encountered which effectively halts training since progress can only be made if the error is reduced which is not possible in the neighbourhood of a local minimum. In such cases training needs to be restarted from a different set of initial weights, or possibly a new network architecture used. A second problem with network learning is overtraining. If a network is overtrained it tends to *memorise* the training pattern - target output pairs, and as a result does not create a general mapping of the vectors. Consequently, it does not perform well when presented with previously unseen patterns. As an example of overtraining consider a one input network trained to approximate the function given by the data presented in figure 7.13. With sufficient hidden nodes the network is able to exactly classify each of the 10 training patterns, as indicated by the solid line. However, the underlying function, represented by the dotted line would be the desired mapping and would result in a better generalisation performance.

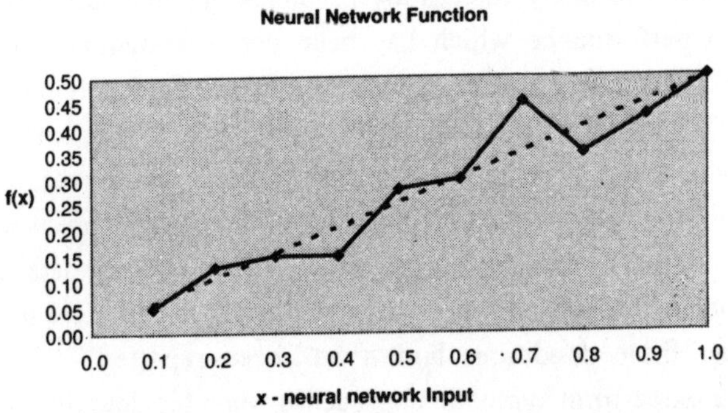

Neural Network Function

Figure 7.13: Over-fitted data

In summary, feedforward neural networks consist of many weighted connections which link the input layer, via the hidden nodes to the output layer. The *knowledge* possessed by the system, gained from training, is represented by these weights together with the activation function, which constitute the mapping from the input patterns to the outputs and is therefore distributed. Consequently, these networks are not easy to interpret, and explanation is not readily available, and, unlike linear regression models (which also represent knowledge in numerical values), the non-linearity introduced by the activation functions adds further complexity to the form of the network. However, they do provide an effective means of establishing non-linear mappings.

Why Use Neural Networks for Forecasting?

The desire to predict future events, or as Casti[13] elegantly states 'to push back the shadow of ignorance', coupled with the integration of computing technology in business environments, led to an explosion of forecasting techniques throughout the second half of the 20th century. Computationally intensive statistical techniques can be performed within fractions of a second with modern day computers and are therefore prevalent throughout the business world. Expert systems have become more widespread in offices, and in recent years neural network forecasting methods have also started to increase in popularity.

Although unable to explain and justify their output, neural networks offer an appealing solution to many forecasting problems, mainly due to their good generalisation performance which has been demonstrated in a variety of domains. Neural networks are, in principle, capable of solving any non-linear classification problem which illustrates the degree of flexibility associated with these systems. Although statistical techniques have been used with high levels of success for many forecasting problems, these methods are often very data dependent, with noisy or missing data leading to erroneous conclusions. Neural networks, on the other hand, are much more tolerant under these conditions and it has been reported[14,15] that these systems often outperform symbolic approaches when the domain information is incomplete or contains noisy data. Although neural networks can be likened to unconstrained non-linear regression, Refenes et al[16] assert that in their field of study, stock performance modelling, neural networks represent the domain more convincingly than regression models. This improved performance over regression models was also found in a credit card fraud problem[17], where the author reports that the neural network approach proved to be much more successful than traditional regression analysis.

Many other studies have demonstrated equally impressive results in forecasting environments. For example, with respect to bankruptcy prediction, Wilson and Sharda[18] report that a neural network trained on five economic ratios outperformed discriminant analysis in prediction accuracy, and that the networks offered a significant improvement in prediction accuracy compared to chance.

A further advantage with neural network models compared to traditional modelling techniques is their ability to reveal undiscovered non-linear relationships between the input parameters. This attribute is especially relevant when little domain knowledge is available, or the complex relationships between the variables are poorly understood. It has been well documented that a major drawback to the development of expert systems is the difficulty associated with the knowledge acquisition phase. The process of acquiring expert knowledge for a domain can be very time consuming, depending as it does on analyses of relevant literature and interviews with human experts. Although a limited degree of domain knowledge is desirable prior to neural network development (i.e. to ensure the relevant data is incorporated into the network) the task of modelling the domain is undertaken by the network itself during training. Hence, the use of neural networks in data mining problems. The elimination of the time consuming, and complex, phase of development is a significant advantage to the system developer.

Even in environments where known rules form the basis of expert decision-making, it is sometimes difficult to specify the complete process the experts follow for marginal cases. An example domain is mortgage assessment. Collins, Ghosh and Scofield[19] trained a neural network on several thousand underwriter judgements and report that the network achieved a good level of agreement with experts in the domain. Therefore, the system represented the knowledge of several different underwriters (experts). Since these experts were located in different parts of the country which affected their decisions, the network also incorporated an element of geographical knowledge. When disagreement did occur, it was for marginal cases where a high degree of disagreement also existed among the experts.

An additional example of neural networks outperforming human experts is found in stock market forecasting problems. Fishman, Barr and Loick[20] report that a network trained on economic indicators performed better than the experts using the same data. Other stock trading successes have been reported by Collard[21], where a commodity trading network returned higher profits than other trading strategies, and in the work of Kamijo and Tanigawa[22] where the network was more successful than a 'buy and hold' strategy for the Tokyo Stock Exchange.

Clearly, neural networks have much to offer the field of forecasting, especially in domains with a large volume of example cases. In well defined domains where the knowledge can be represented in rule form, such as game playing and tasks involving technical expertise, the symbolic paradigm offers the most obvious solution. However, in less well structured domains containing a potentially unlimited number of possibly relevant facts, the relationships between which are unclear, the connectionist approach is often preferable.

Development of a Neural Network

In this section the neural network approach is applied to the horseracing problem. All stages of network development are addressed from data representation to testing and evaluation.

As with other forms of models, the neural network can be applied to all, or part, of the problem domain, providing sufficient data are available. For instance, it is possible to generate neural network models that are applicable to different race types, such as handicaps as opposed non-handicaps, or different horse types, such as outsiders or favourites. For this example non-juvenile pattern races have been chosen as the domain and the methods outlined in Chapter 3 have been used to generate any intermediate conclusions such as going suitability and fitness.

Data Representation

Five critical factors of the animal's profile constitute the training and testing vectors, namely: speed rating, going suitability, distance suitability, fitness and trainer's success rate. The aim of the network is to discriminate between race winners and losers therefore, the target value is the finishing position reduced to a binary form (i.e. 1 for a winner, 0 for a loser). Many other variables could have been used in the training and testing patterns and as the target value. For example, the race time could replace the finishing position as the target output, or distance beaten by the winner. The training patterns could also have included such variables as age or jockey's ability. As with the knowledge-based approach the question of within-race competition needs to be addressed after the network output has been derived using the principles outlines in Chapter 4.

As mentioned previously, input data representation can have a significant effect on the network's performance and as such many different representations were tested during the development of this network. The most difficult variable to represent in the system is the ability rating, in this case the speed rating. The normalising procedure previously discussed (Chapter 3) was adopted, and in order to address the scaling and missing data problems three input nodes were used. As an example consider figure 7.14. The three input nodes are used to represent separately the scaled rating, the difference between the highest and second highest rated horses in a race and a missing rating.

Horse	Ability Rating	Neural Network Inputs		
		Scaled	Best	Missing
1	144	4	0	0
2	148	0	4	0
3	125	23	0	0
4	110	38	0	0
5	No rating	148	0	1

Figure 7.14: Representing the speed rating

For normalisation, upper and lower bounds of 50 and 0 were used. Consequently, a scaled speed rating of 25 would be represented in the network as (0.5,0,0), a top rated horse 25lbs clear of the next best would be input as (0,0.5,0) and a missing rating as (1,0,1). It is possible to train a network on this one factor to see how it is mapped to the output. As an example, a 3-5-1 network was trained on the pattern race data for just the ability rating; the outputs generated are presented in figures 7.15 for scaled speed figures and 7.16 for the difference between the highest and second highest scaled speed ratings. A missing rating produced an output of 0.08,

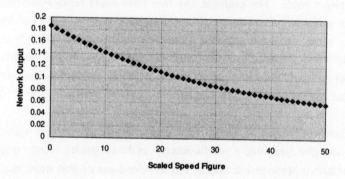

Figure 7.15: Neural network response to speed figures (input 1)

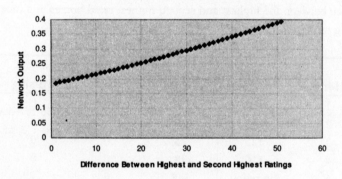

Figure 7.16: Neural network response to speed figures (input 2)

implying a likely loser.

The output presented in figure 7.15 for the scaled speed figures is clearly non-linear and decreases as the rating increases, as expected. After all the higher the rating the more the horse needs to improve in terms of ability to match the highest rated horse. Figure 7.16 appears more linear with the chance of success increasing as the difference increases. Again this is to be expected and illustrates the value of the speed figures. It should be remembered that, unlike in the knowledge-based approach, the network is not directed to give the higher rated horses more chance of success and before training it possesses no knowledge of the domain. Instead it *learns* this knowledge for itself from the example cases. The speed figure network is very simplistic in form and it is not difficult to associate chance of success with a higher rating. However, networks also learn more complex, multi-variable, relationships in more involved systems. These relationships may not have been identified by the domain experts or considered by the model developer and as a consequence would be omitted from a knowledge-based model.

Representing the remainder of the inputs was less complex. The going and distance suitability inputs both required just one binary input which could be switched from 0 (unsuitable) to 1 for suitable for each factor. The fitness factor can take one of three values: -1, 0, or 1, representing *unfit*, *doubtful fitness* and *fit*. Three binary inputs were used to represent this factor as follows:

		inputs	
Fitness -1:	1	0	0
Fitness 0:	0	1	0
Fitness 1:	0	0	1

To represent the trainer's success rate in the network a single real-valued input was used, with zero equating to a success rate of 0% and 1 a success rate of 100%.

Although these five factors formed the knowledge of the network, it was supplemented with a rank of the speed figure to indicate the position of the horse in terms of ability with respect to the other runners. The ranks are easily derived, with the top rated horse ranked 1, the next best 2, and so on. This information required one further real-valued input and is normalised by subtracting 1 (the lowest rank) and dividing by 24, the difference between the lowest rank and largest field size in all of the training races.

The final architecture required 10 input nodes, (three for the speed figures, one each for the going and distance suitability variables, three for the fitness measure, one for the trainer's success rate and one for the rank of the speed figure). Eight hidden nodes were used in one hidden layer and one output node. Consequently, there were 97 weighted connections (including the biases).

Network Training and Testing

Network training is an iterative process: networks are trained, tested and either retained or discarded. There are different ways to determine when training should be suspended (i.e. using the mean squared error or a separate test set) and for this example the test set approach was adopted. Training of the neural network was periodically halted, its performance checked against the test set, and training resumed. The training set consisted of approximately 850 example race performances representing 100 races; the test set comprised 55 races with a total of 450 runners. Many different architectures were tested for the horseracing problem together with various data representations before the network presented in this section was developed.

The aim of the horseracing network is to discriminate between race winners and losers. Therefore, any performance measure should be based on this statistic. It is possible to gauge the accuracy of the system by comparing the output of the network against known values for patterns not included in the training set. Using the sigmoid activation function produces a real-valued output from the network in contrast to the binary target value associated with the training and test patterns. In many applications it is possible to set a threshold value on the output of the network, say 0.5, and then compare the recoded binary outputs with the known target values. However, with this domain the within-race competition complicates the process, since it would be possible to have several horses classified as winners in one race. Therefore, an alternative procedure needs to be considered. The obvious method is to associate the most likely winner of the race with the horse possessing the highest network output.

For the 55 test races, the network correctly identified 17 winners, a success rate of almost 31%, this compares to a random expectation of just 14.1%. A level £1 stake placed on each of the 55 selections would have yielded an average return of 46p per bet at starting price. These results are very encouraging and demonstrate the utility of neural networks in the horseracing domain. Further evaluation of this method is undertaken in Chapter 8.

Analysing the Network

A crucial aspect of many decision making situations is the ability to interpret and assess the quality of the advice which informs the decision. It has long been acknowledged that the utility of expert systems as decision support tools depends very much on their ability to explain and justify their advice. However, a major drawback of neural networks is that their knowledge and expertise is encoded implicitly across sets of numerical weights. This implicit knowledge is therefore not directly available to aid the interpretation and assessment of network output. The inability of neural networks to explain and justify themselves is a severe limitation in their application to decision support. Recent approaches to explaining the output of neural networks include the use of rule extraction which attempts to make explicit the relationships between input parameters and trained network responses. Several algorithms for extracting rules from trained neural networks have been proposed, for example the *Box Rule* method developed by Howes and Crook[23]. However the same authors have also developed methods for estimating the influence of the individual input variables on the network and it is these methods which are considered in this section.

Three measures of input parameter influence have been developed: an assessment of the *general influence* of each input parameter; the *specific influence* of individual input parameters on the results of network queries; and the *potential influence* of each input parameter on the response of the network. The general influence measure ranks the input parameters in order of *importance*, information which can be verified by human experts on the completion of network training. For a given network query, the specific influence indicates which of the input variables is contributing most to the output of the network, and whether this contribution is supportive or inhibitory. The user would therefore be made aware of situations where the output depended heavily on a small number of the inputs. Finally, the potential influence metric indicates the *power* of each input parameter. In other words, it expresses the capability of each input variable to change the output of the network. This information would assume greater importance if the input variables were subject to measurement error, or thought to be uncertain to some degree. These measures are discussed in this section.

The influence measures depend on an examination of the network's weights and therefore figure 7.17 has been included to clarify the notation.

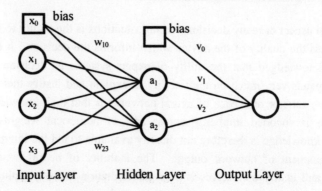

Figure 7.17: Notation for the feedforward neural network

General Influence

With linear regression modelling it is possible to discern directly from the regression equation the relative effect of each variable and whether it is positively or negatively correlated with the dependent variable. For instance, a linear regression model used to predict the likely success of university applicants would probably suggest that the likely level of success of an applicant is positively correlated with school examination results. Clearly, this will not hold true in all cases, it is merely a generalisation. In terms of effect each coefficient of a linear regression equation represents the change in the output of the function associated with a unit change in the corresponding input. Providing the inputs have been scaled to a uniform range the importance of each input is easily determined from a direct comparison of the coefficients. For non-standardised data the range of each input would need to be considered before comparison. However, this does make the assumption that the inputs are independent. The true importance of two dependent inputs would not necessarily be apparent from this type of comparison.

For neural networks it is not possible to indicate the correlations of each input parameter due to the non-linear nature of the network. However, it is possible to generate an estimate of the general level of influence exhibited by each parameter from an analysis of the network weights. For feedforward networks with n input nodes, one hidden layer with h nodes and one output node the General Influence (GI) of the ith component of the input vector can be defined as follows:

$$GI(i) = \frac{\sum_{j=1}^{h} \left| \dfrac{w_{ji}}{\sum_{k=0}^{n} |w_{jk}|} \cdot v_j \right|}{\sum_{j=0}^{h} |v_j|} \qquad i = 1,2,..n \qquad (7.3)$$

where w_{ji} is the weight from ith input node to the jth hidden node and v_j is the weight from the jth hidden node to the output node. Biases are given the subscript 0. The importance of the bias can be determined by difference, i.e.

$$GI(0) = 1 - \sum_{i=1}^{n} GI(x_i) \qquad (7.4)$$

Equation 7.3 is simply compounded weighted averages and is independent of the activation function, therefore it is applicable to networks trained on all activation functions which are monotonically increasing. Unlike linear regression models it is not possible to generate a level of importance by simply considering the weight which acts directly on the input value. A large input-to-hidden layer weight does not necessarily imply an equivalent significant effect on the output of the network due to the other layers of weights. Consequently, it is necessary to consider compounded weights which account for the difference between the weights in the various layers of the network

GI values can be calculated for each input parameter and displayed to the user. However, it should be noted that these measures are independent of the actual value of the input patterns, and therefore can only provide an overview of the influences which may differ for specific input patterns.

For the horseracing network the general influence values presented in figure 7.18 can be calculated. From this table it can be seen that the speed rating variable is represented by four inputs to the network: *speed rating, top speed rating, no speed rating and rank of speed rating*. This corresponds to the data representation discussed previously. Similarly the fitness variable is

Input Variable	General Influence
Speed Rating	7.0%
Top Speed Rating	10.5%
No Speed Rating	5.7%
Going Suitability	4.1%
Distance Suitability	5.3%
Unfit	4.5%
Fitness Unknown	6.2%
Fitness OK	2.5%
Trainers Strike Rate	25.2%
Rank of Speed Figure	15.6%
Bias	*13.4%*

Figure 7.18: General influence for horseracing network

represented by three inputs. From the influences it appears that the most important input is the trainers strike rate (25.2%). However, the speed figure is divided into four inputs which although singularly are considered less influential than the trainer's strike rate, combined they are of greater importance. It is interesting to note the low levels of influence associated with the other variables (between 2% and 7% each) implying that the network could possibly be pruned and these inputs removed. One surprising fact is the low influence for the *Fitness OK* input, less than both the other fitness inputs.

Specific Influence

For purposes of explanation it is preferable to attach a level of importance to the various elements of the information on which a decision is based. For instance, when diagnosing specific diseases there may be several symptoms which contribute to the overall diagnosis. Associated with these symptoms will be varying degrees of correlation with a range of diseases: for instance, the presence of spots and the diseases chicken pox and measles. When confirming the diagnosis, the specialist (expert) is able to list the symptoms on which his/her conclusions have been drawn. Normally, these symptoms will be presented in order, with the most significant first, with some superfluous findings omitted from the justification. Although this is covered in-part by maximally general rules[23] the ranking of the other variables in terms of causal importance does not form part of rule extraction algorithms. Calculating the specific influence of an input parameter facilitates this ranking by attaching a numerical level of importance to each input.

For individual input patterns it is possible to be more precise regarding the influence of an input parameter, and to determine whether it is supporting or inhibiting the network's decision. It is possible to generate the degree to which each input parameter contributes to the output of the network (its *specific influence*), by iteratively replacing each input value with zero and re-interrogating the network, recording the difference the change makes to the summed contribution at the network's output node. These differences can then be normalised. Therefore, for a known input vector the specific influences, $SI_i(x)$, of each input component can be determined from equation 7.5.

$$SI_i(\mathbf{x}) = \frac{f^{-1}(net(\mathbf{x})) - f^{-1}(net(\mathbf{x}'_i))}{\sum_{k=1}^{n} \left| f^{-1}(net(\mathbf{x})) - f^{-1}(net(\mathbf{x}'_k)) \right| + \left| SI_0(\mathbf{x}) \right|} \tag{7.5}$$

where $SI_0(\mathbf{x}) = f^{-1}(net(\mathbf{x})) - \sum_{k=1}^{n} \left[f^{-1}(net(\mathbf{x})) - f^{-1}(net(\mathbf{x}'_k)) \right]$ (7.6)

where $\mathbf{x}$ is the original input pattern, $\mathbf{x}'_k$ represents the input vector with the kth component replaced with zero, f is the network's activation function and the subscript zero refers to the bias.

These specific influence measures can be presented together with the output of the network illustrating the contribution of each input parameter. For the horseracing network the normalised pattern

$$\{0.00, 0.06, 0.00, 1.00, 1.00, 0.00, 0.00, 1.00, 0.33, 0.00\}$$

produced a network output of 0.3198 and the specific influences given in figure 7.19. From this table it can be seen that the horse under consideration is top rated on speed figures, 3lbs higher than the next best runner. The horse is fit, suited by going and distance and its trainer has a very high success rate, 33.3%. Zero input parameters necessarily have zero specific

Input Variable	Input Value[†]	Specific Influence
Speed Rating	0	0.00
Top Speed Rating	3	1.09
No Speed Rating	0	0.00
Going Suitability	1	-5.76
Distance Suitability	1	3.74
Unfit	0	0.00
Fitness Unknown	0	0.00
Fitness OK	1	0.12
Trainers Strike Rate	33.3	70.37
Rank of Speed Fig.	1	0.00
Bias	-	-18.93

[†] Input values before normalisation

Figure 7.19: Specific influences for a likely winner

influence (in other words an input of zero has no effect on the output of the network), however, the trainer's success rate has a significant influence on the output, accounting for 70% of the total influence in fact. Interestingly, the going suitability input is inhibiting the output even though the horse is suited by the ground. This appears anomalous since reducing this input to zero, indicating that the horse is not definitely suited by the going, actually increases the output of the network making the horse a stronger selection. This may result from a biased training set, or merely be due to the non-linearity in the network with a different input pattern producing a positive influence for the going variable.

Input Variable	Input Value[†]	Specific Influence
Speed Rating	40	-12.77
Top Speed Rating	0	0.00
No Speed Rating	0	0.00
Going Suitability	0	0.00
Distance Suitability	1	6.43
Unfit	1	-10.31
Fitness Unknown	0	0.00
Fitness OK	0	0.00
Trainers Strike Rate	5.0	9.61
Rank of Speed Fig.	20	-39.05
Bias	-	-21.83

[†] Input values before normalisation

Figure 7.20: Specific influences for a likely loser

As a second example consider the specific influences given in figure 7.20 for a pattern which generates a network output of 0.0151. On the plus side the network output is positively influence by the trainer's success rate and the distance suitability variable. However, there are several inhibitory inputs, namely the speed rating, the fitness variable (because the horse is unfit) and the rank of the speed figure. Clearly, this horse has little chance of success.

Potential Influence

The specific influence possessed by an input variable is different from its *potential influence* on the network's decision. The potential influence indicates the parameter's possible effect on the output. For instance, for a given input pattern, an input component may have very low specific influence on the output but high potential influence. In other words, such an input would have the potential to significantly change the output of the network. In order to calculate the potential influence of a particular component (x_t), it is necessary to constrain the remaining input parameters at their respective pattern values whilst allowing x_t to vary over its valid range. The potential influence is the range given by the maximum and minimum values of the network's output under the new constraints.

For a two layer feedforward network (i.e. one hidden layer) with n input nodes and h hidden nodes and one output node, the network mapping function can be defined as:

$$net(\mathbf{x}) = f\left(v_0 + \sum_{j=1}^{h} a_j(\mathbf{x}) \cdot v_j\right) \quad (7.7)$$

where f is the activation function and $a_j(\mathbf{x})$ is the activation of the jth hidden node, v_j is the weight from the jth hidden node to the output node and,

$$a_j(\mathbf{x}) = f\left(w_{j0} + \sum_{i=1}^{n} x_i \cdot w_{ji}\right) \quad (7.8)$$

w_{ji} is the weight from ith input node to the jth hidden node. By isolating one of the input components, x_t, equation 7.7 can be rewritten as:

$$net(\mathbf{x}) = f\left(v_0 + \sum_{j=1}^{h}\left(v_j \cdot f\left(w_{j0} + \sum_{\substack{j=1 \\ j \neq t}}^{n} x_j \cdot w_{ji} + x_t \cdot w_{jt}\right)\right)\right) \quad (7.9)$$

Equation 7.9 can be viewed as a single variable formula in x_t which, for the sigmoid activation function, can easily be graphed or differentiated. The level of potential influence (PI) for the input parameter x_t for the input pattern $\mathbf{x}$ becomes:

$$PI_t(\mathbf{x}, net) = \left[\min_{x_t}(net(\mathbf{x})), \max_{x_t}(net(\mathbf{x}))\right] \quad (7.10)$$

The potential influence is essentially a measure of the variability, or sensitivity, of the input component.

Finding the maxima and minima of equation 7.9 can be achieved using one of several applicable numerical algorithms, such as a Variable Metric Method. Although these methods require the calculation of derivatives, this is not a problem since equation 7.9 is easily differentiable.

The potential influence of each parameter provides the user with valuable information. For example an input query producing a network output of 0.0672 for the horseracing network is displayed with its potential influences in figure 7.21.

Input Variable	Input Value[†]	Potential Influence
Speed Rating	30	0.05 - 0.10
Top Speed Rating	0	0.07 - 0.17
No Speed Rating	0	0.07 - 0.10
Going Suitability	1	0.07 - 0.08
Distance Suitability	1	0.06 - 0.07
Unfit	0	0.05 - 0.07
Fitness Unknown	0	0.04 - 0.07
Fitness OK	1	0.06 - 0.07
Trainers Strike Rate	11.0	0.03 - 0.24
Rank of Speed Fig.	4	0.02 - 0.08

[†] Input values before normalisation

Figure 7.21: Potential influences for a likely winner

From figure 7.21 the potential influence of each input can be deduced. As in the case of the general influence measure, the going, distance and fitness variables have little effect on the output of the network with at best an increase of the network output to 0.08 achievable by altering any of these inputs. However, the trainer's success rate and speed figures are capable of significantly changing the network's output to a value of 0.24 in the case of the former. Again this corresponds with the findings of the other influence measures.

When the network contains data with high degrees of uncertainty the potential influence of each input becomes particularly informative. For example, data items subject to measurement error such as temperature, or estimated data such as the weight of an object. In these cases it may not be possible to ascertain the exact temperature or weight and therefore the accuracy of each input would be uncertain. Input components about which the user is unsure of the correct value become more critical if they exhibit a high degree of influence on the output. For instance, the age of a patient may be important in a medical diagnosis. If, for some reason, this information is unavailable and needs to be estimated the potential influence of the age input will indicate whether an incorrect estimate will significantly effect the conclusions of the network. However, the potential influence does not directly inform the user of the stability of the network output in the neighbourhood of the query point. It merely expresses the potential of each input over its entire range.

Artificial neural networks have been employed to solve problems in a wide range of domains, however it is generally accepted that without explanatory information to support their output, connectionist systems will be limited in their application, especially in domains in which it is necessary to understand the learned concepts, for instance in data mining problems. Consequently, the investigation of methods similar to those in this section which provide an insight into the network's mapping function, the reliability and accuracy of its output, and the significance of the input values is a natural, and important, step towards generating a comprehensive explanation facility.

References

1   *An Introduction to Neural Computing*, by I. Aleksander and H. Morton, published by Chapman and Hall, London, England, 1991.

2   *Psychology (Briefer Course)*, by W. James, Holt, New York, U.S.A., 1890.

3   *A Logical Calculus of Ideas Imminent in Nervous Activity*, by W.S. McCulloch and W. Pitts, in Bulletin of Mathematical Biophysics, Vol. 5, pp115-133, 1943.

4   *The Organization of Behavior*, by D. Hebb, published by Wiley, New York, U.S.A., 1949.

5   *The Perceptron: A Probabilistic Model for Information Storage and Organization in the Brain*, by F. Rosenblatt, in Psychological Review, Vol. 65, pp386-407, 1958.

6   *Adaptive Switching Circuits*, by B. Widrow and M. E. Hoff, in 1969 IRE WESCON Convention Record: Part 4, Computers: Man-Machine Systems, Los Angeles, CA, U.S.A., 1960.

7   *Perceptrons*, by M. Minsky and S. Papert, published by MIT Press, Cambridge, MA, U.S.A., 1969.

8   *Learning Representations by Back-Propagating Errors*, by D. E. Rumelhart, G. E. Hinton and R. J. Williams, in Nature, 1986

9   *Beyond Regression*, by P. Werbos, PhD Thesis, Harvard University, Cambridge, MA, U.S.A., 1974.

10 *Learning Logic*, by D. B. Parker, Invention Report S81-64, file1, Office of Technology Licensing, Stanford University, U.S.A., 1982

11 *Self-Organization and Associative Memory*, by T. Kohonen, Spronger-Verlag, Berlin, Germany, 1984.

12 *Computational Intelligence PC Tools*, by R.C. Eberhart, P.K. Simpson and R.C. Dobbins, published by Academic Press Limited, London, England, 1996.

13 *Searching For Certainty - what science can know about the future*, by J. L. Casti, Scribners, London, England, 1992.

14 *An Empirical Comparison of ID3 and Back-Propagation*, by D.H. Fisher and K.B. McKusick, in Proceedings of IJCAI-89, (Detroit), pp788-793, Morgan Kaufman, Los Altos, Ca, U.S.A., 1989

15 *An Experimental Comparison of Symbolic and Connectionist Learning Algorithms*, by R. Mooney, J.W. Shavlik, G.G. Towell and A. Gove, in Proceedings of IJCAI-89 (Detroit), pp775-780, Morgan Kaufman, Los Altos, Ca, U.S.A., 1989

16 *Stock Performance Modeling Using Neural Networks: A Comparative Study With Regression Models*, by A.N. Refenes, A. Zapranis and G. Francis, in Neural Networks, Vol. 7, No. 2, pp375-388, 1994.

[17] *New Business Uses for Neurocomputing*, by J. Rochester, in I/S Analyzer, Feb. 1990.

[18] *Bankruptcy Prediction Using Neural Networks*, by R.L. Wilson and R. Sharda, in Decision Support Systems, 1994.

[19] *An Application of a Multiple Neural Network Learning System to Emulation of Mortgage Underwriting Judgements*, by E. Collins, S. Ghosh and C.L. Scofield, in IEEE International Conference on Neural Networks, San Diego, CA, U.S.A., pp458-466, 1988.

[20] *Using Neural Networks*, by M. Fishman, D. Barr and W. Loick, in Market Analysis, Technical Analysis of Stocks and Commodities, pp18-25, Apr. 1991.

[21] *Commodity Trading with a Neural Net*, by J.E. Collard, in Neural Network News, Vol. 2, No. 10, Oct. 1990.

[22] *Stock Price Pattern Recognition: A Recurrent Neural Network Approach*, by K. Kamijo and T. Tanigawa, in International Conference on Neural Networks, San Diego, Ca, U.S.A., June 1990.

[23] *Efficient Rule Extraction from Real-Valued Feedforward Neural Networks*, by P. J. Howes and N. T. Crook, in Proceedings of Eighth Ireland Conference on Artificial Intelligence (AI-97), University of Ulster, Northern Ireland, September 1997.

8

Applying the Techniques

In this chapter the forecasting methods proposed in the earlier chapters are applied to several races taken from the 1998 season. These races are considered in detail with the specific aim of illustrating the strengths and weakness of the techniques. For each race the horse profiles are presented together with the output of the relevant models, such as the knowledge-based approach, the reference class method and the neural network. A summary of the selections highlighted by the rule-based methods presented in Chapter 5 is given in appendix A5.

The racecard given for each race includes the following information: race name (abbreviated), race distance, horse number, horse name, age, weight carried in stones and pounds excluding jockey's allowance or overweight, trainer, and jockey. For the horse profiles the following key is provided: *RPH* - Raceform Private Handicap rating, *SF* - Speed Figure, *Going* - going suitability, *Dist.* - distance suitability, *TSR* - trainer's strike rate[†] , *W-R* - number of wins and runs.

For the contents of the profile table the following abbreviations are used:
- ✗ - no proven form when used for going or distance suitability factors, when used for fitness it means that the horse is unlikely to be fit.
- ? - is used when a factor cannot be evaluated, i.e. fitness is doubtful.
- ✓ - proven form over the distance or on the going, or fitness assured.

[†] The trainer's strike rate depends on the age of the horse and its experience. Three ratios are used: for juvenile debutants, juveniles which have raced and non-juveniles.

Kempton 11 April 1998　　　　　　　　Going: Soft

No	Horse	Age and Weight	Trainer	Jockey
Milcars Stanmore Conditions Stakes				*1m 2f Jub*
1	**Scorned**	3 9-4	I A Balding	S Whitworth
2	**Benin**	3 8-13	H R A Cecil	K Fallon
3	**Last Christmas**	3 8-13	B W Hills	Pat Eddery
4	**Mantusis**	3 8-13	P W Harris	O Peslier

Starting Prices: 9/4 Scorned, 9/4 Mantusis, 3/1 Benin, 4/1 Last Christmas

Horse Profiles

Horse	RPH	SF	Going	Dist.	Fit	TSR	W-R
Scorned	116+	79	✗	✗	✓	12.0	2-3
Benin	104+	75	✗	✗	?	20.4	1-1
Last Christmas	98	66	✗	✗	?	12.7	1-2
Mantusis	102	49	✗	✗	?	10.1	1-2

Forecast

An early season conditions race featuring horses with potential and as yet unexposed. In fact, it is very difficult to be confident about any factors of the horse profiles. None of the horses have encountered the soft going before nor raced over the trip, and the ratings are very suspect given the limited number of races on which they are based. The knowledge-based system is appropriate to this race type with the following forecasts made:

Horse	KBS Output	Fair Odds
Scorned	24.1	2/1
Benin	20.9	3/1
Last Christmas	19.3	4/1
Mantusis	20.4	10/3

From the forecasts this appears to be a very tight race, however, the closeness of the prices merely reflects the lack of reliable data about any of the runners. Essentially, the knowledge-based system differentiates between the runners purely on the ratings. Based on the forecast though, Scorned offered a reasonable betting opportunity at $9/_4$.

Race Result: 1st Scorned, 2nd Last Christmas, 3rd Mantusis

Kempton 11 April 1998   Going: Soft

Milcars Easter Stakes (Listed Race)			**1m Jub**
No *Horse*	*Age and Weight*	*Trainer*	*Jockey*
1 **Chester House**	3 8-8	H R A Cecil	K Fallon
2 **Dahomey**	3 8-8	C E Brittain	Pat Eddery
3 **Gurkha**	3 8-8	R Hannon	Dane O'Neill
4 **Krispy Knight**	3 8-8	J W Hills	R Hills

Starting Prices: 11/10 Chester House, 15/8 Gurkha, 6/1 Krispy Knight, 8/1 Dahomey

Horse Profiles

Horse	RPH	SF	Going	Dist.	Fit	TSR	W-R
Chester House	126	69	✗	✗	?	22.4	1-2
Dahomey	74	81	✗	✗	?	8.6	0-1
Gurkha	111	66	✗	✗	?	9.4	1-2
Krispy Knight	101	62	✗	✗	✓	10.7	1-4

Forecast

Another race greatly affected by the soft going. Chester House is made favourite mainly on reputation and the fact that he is trained by Henry Cecil. No horses are proven on the going or over the trip, with only Krispy Knight guaranteed to be fit after a recent race. Another disconcerting fact is the marked difference between the two sets of ratings. Whilst Dahomey has produced the highest speed figure he is rated far lower than his three opponents on form figures. A Listed race of this type is applicable to both the neural network and knowledge-based methods, resulting in two forecasts.

Horse	NN Output	NN Odds	KBS Output	KBS Odds
Chester House	0.05	4/1	24.1	6/4
Dahomey	0.07	2/1	12.4	8/1
Gurkha	0.04	5/1	20.1	3/1
Krispy Knight	0.07	9/4	17.4	4/1

The importance of the rating is clearly illustrated by the outputs from the two models, with Dahomey rated a $^2/_1$ chance by the neural network (which is based on speed ratings) and an $^8/_1$ chance by the knowledge-based system which uses form figures. At their respective prices neither Chester House nor Gurkha could be backed, however, using the neural network forecast Dahomey presents an outstanding bet at $^8/_1$ (early morning price an even better $^{14}/_1$) and so too does Krispy Knight at $^6/_1$. The knowledge-based method indicates that Dahomey is fairly priced but, like the neural network, predicts that Krispy Knight is overpriced.

Race Result: *1st Krispy Knight, 2nd Gurkha, 3rd Dahomey*

Newcastle 13 April 1998   Going: Soft

Brighton Races Novice Stakes				**5f**
No *Horse*	*Age and Weight*	*Trainer*		*Jockey*
1 **Principality**	2 8-12	J Berry		K Darley
2 **Beryl The Peril**	2 8-7	N Bycroft		S Maloney
3 **Brave Indian**	2 8-7	M Brittain		M Byrne
4 **Lady Nairn**	2 8-7	J J Quinn		J Fortune
5 **Pennymoor**	2 8-7	M Johnston		J Carroll
6 **Saphire**	2 8-7	C B B Booth		A Culhane

Starting Prices: 4/9 Principality, 9/2 Pennymoor, 5/1 Lady Nairn, 14/1 Saphire, 20/1 Brave Girl, 50/1 Beryl The Peril

Horse Profiles

Horse	RPH	SF	Going	Dist.	Fit	TSR	W-R
Principality	-	67	?	✓	✓	14.6	0-1
Beryl The Peril	-	-	?	✗	✗	0.0	0-0
Brave Indian	-	-	?	✗	✗	0.0	0-0
Lady Nairn	-	-	?	✗	?	6.3	0-0
Pennymoor	-	-	?	✗	?	13.0	0-0
Saphire	-	-	?	✗	✗	0.0	0-0

Forecast

A difficult early season two-year-old race to assess with only one horse having raced before, namely Principality. Race experience tends to be very valuable in this type of race especially on soft ground where stamina is at a premium. Furthermore, Principality is the only colt in the field, hence the extra weight carried. Given that Principality has previously raced, is proven on the ground and over the distance, trained by top two-year-old trainer Jack Berry and is guaranteed to be fit, ensures favouritism. Pennymoor from the strong Mark Johnston stable is a possible danger. The reference class method is used for this race.

Horse	RC Output	Fair Odds
Principality	14.9	10/11
Beryl The Peril	1.4	20/1
Brave Indian	1.4	20/1
Lady Nairn	4.2	6/1
Pennymoor	6.1	4/1
Saphire	0.7	33/1

Form the forecast Principality is clearly expected to win, however, a starting price of $^4/_9$ is far too short. Pennymoor could be backed at $^9/_2$ as well as the outsider, Beryl The Peril.

Race Result: *1st Principality, 2nd Saphire, 3rd Lady Nairn*

Interestingly, Principality's winning margin was only a neck from Saphire with the race in doubt until the last few strides, hardly the superiority expected from a long odds on chance.

Newmarket 3 May 1998   Going: Good

Newmarket Challenge Whip (Maiden)			1m Rowley Mile
No Horse	*Age and Weight*	*Trainer*	*Jockey*
1 **Rajati**	3 9-0	Mrs J Cecil	Martin Dwyer
2 **High Demand**	3 8-9	B W Hills	M Hills
Starting Prices: 1/4 High Demand, 2/1 Rajati			

Horse Profiles

Horse	RPH	SF	Going	Dist.	Fit	TSR	W-R
Rajati	72	65	✗	✗	✓	13.6	0-4
High Demand	-	-	✗	✗	?	12.7	0-0

Forecast

In the age of competitive racing it is quite amazing that the conditions of this race have not been changed. Year after year the race produces two or three runners at best which is hardly surprising when one considers the race conditions. *The Whip* is restricted to horses that are owned by the 530 Jockey Club and Jockey Club Rooms members and the only justification for the continuation of this ridiculous event is *tradition*. Similarly, it is also surprising that the Jockey Club remains given the introduction of the BHB some years ago. After all what do the Jockey Club members actually contribute to racing, does anyone know?

The race itself features a gelding, Rajati, which has raced four times and failed to reach the frame and an unraced Sabrehill filly. With a form figure in the low 70's Rajati is clearly no world beater however he is fit and his trainer has a reasonable success rate at 13.6%. The knowledge-based system produced the following output:

Horse	KBS Output	Fair Odds
Rajati	24.1	2/7
High Demand	12.4	7/2

Paradoxically, it is the main weakness of the knowledge-based system that enables it to correctly identify the winner. The advantage that Rajati holds over High Demand is the fact that it is rated, and with only two runners is necessarily top rated. The rating has significant influence on the system which result in Rajati considered to be a near certainty, with associated odds of $^2/_7$.

Race Result: *1st Rajati, 2nd High Demand*

Salisbury 3 May 1998   Going: Good to Soft

Hatherden Maiden Stakes			**1m 2f**
No Horse	Age and Weight	Trainer	Jockey
1 **Banker Dwerry**	3 9-0	S P C Woods	A Clark
2 **Belcade**	3 9-0	D R C Elsworth	S Drowne
3 **Churlish Charm**	3 9-0	R Hannon	Dane O'Neill
4 **Inn On The Park**	3 9-0	S Dow	S Sanders
5 **Monet**	3 9-0	P Chapple-Hyam	S Whitworth
6 **Paddy McGoon**	3 9-0	D R C Elsworth	N Pollard
7 **Sun Dancer**	3 9-0	N A Smith	J Bramhill
8 **Heiress of Meath**	3 8-9	M D I Usher	R Price
9 **New Abbey**	3 8-9	H R A Cecil	W Ryan
10 **Poppy Too**	3 8-9	M Channon	Paul Eddery
11 **Rabea**	3 8-9	J L Dunlop	M Rimmer

Starting Prices: 4/5 New Abbey, 5/1 Monet, 6/1 Banker Dwerry, 12/1 Churlish Charm, Poppy Too, 16/1 Paddy McGoon, Rabea, 20/1 Belcade, 33/1 Inn On The Park, Sun Dancer, 50/1 Heiress Of Meath

Horse Profiles

Horse	RPH	SF	Going	Dist.	Fit	TSR	W-R
Banker Dwerry	89	60	✗	✗	✓	12.7	0-3
Belcade	75?	36	✗	✗	✓	10.2	0-2
Churlish Ch'm	52	22	✗	✗	?	9.4	0-1
In On The Park	67d	39	✗	✗	✓	7.6	0-3
Monet	-	-	✗	✗	✓	13.7	0-0
Paddy McGoon	74t	38	✗	✗	✗	10.2	0-2
Sun Dancer	43	16	✗	✗	✓	5.8	0-2
Heiress of M'	62	6	✗	✗	✓	5.7	0-5
New Abbey	-	-	✗	✗	?	22.4	0-0
Poppy Too	61?	60	✗	✗	✓	9.6	0-1
Rabea	69	22	✗	✗	✓	18.1	0-2

Forecast

Although 11 horses are entered the nine which have previously raced look decidedly poor, this is emphasised by the very low form and speed figures. Consequently, the two unraced horses, both from top stables, do not need to be above average to win this race.

Horse	KBS Output	Fair Odds
Banker Dwerry	24.1	5/1
Belcade	20.4	7/1
Churlish Ch'm	14.2	16/1
In On The Park	18.2	9/1
Monet	12.4	20/1
Paddy McGoon	20.1	15/2
Sun Dancer	12.4	20/1
Heiress of M'	16.9	11/1
New Abbey	12.4	20/1
Poppy Too	16.6	11/1
Rabea	18.8	17/2

However, the weakness of the knowledge-based system highlighted by the previous race is clearly demonstrated here with the unraced pair quoted at fair odds of $^{20}/_1$. New Abbey the unraced horse from the Cecil yard actually started the $^4/_5$ favourite and won cosily illustrating the need for the knowledge-based method to account more precisely for unraced horses, the importance of the top training stables and perhaps pedigree.

> **Race Result**: 1st New Abbey, 2nd Churlish Charm, 3rd Banker Dwerry

Newcastle 21 May 1998   Going: Good to Firm

Northern Racing Novice Stakes			*5f*
No Horse	*Age and Weight*	*Trainer*	*Jockey*
1 **Sammal**	2 9-4	J A Glover	J Fortune
2 **Springs Noblequest**	2 8-13	T D Easterby	L Charnock
3 **Double Two**	2 8-12	T D Easterby	R Winston
4 **Rosselli**	2 8-12	J Berry	J Carroll

Starting Prices: 6/4 Rosselli, 2/1 Sammal, Springs Noblequest, 16/1 Double Two

Horse Profiles

Horse	RPH	SF	Going	Dist.	Fit	TSR	W-R
Sammal	84	57	✗	✓	✓	14.5	1-2
Springs Noble'	80	53	✗	✓	✓	9.8	1-2
Double Two	-	-	✗	✗	✗	0.0	0-0
Rosselli	-	-	✗	✗	?	13.7	0-0

Forecast

A four runner juvenile race with two penalised previous winners: the gelding Sammal and the filly Springs Noblequest. Although form figures in the 80's mark these two horses as slightly above average the speed figures are somewhat disappointing implying that the form figures are possibly over-rated. Jack Berry is a master at training two-year-olds and it was no surprise that Rosselli started favourite. The reference class approach was applied to this race and the following output generated:

Horse	RC Output	Odds
Sammal	2.9	7/1
Springs Noble'	0.8	25/1
Double Two	0.8	25/1
Rosselli	19.2	1/4

Although it was no surprise to see Rosselli highlighted as the most likely winner, fair odds of $1/4$ appeared extremely low. A starting price of $6/4$ made Rosselli an outstanding bet and he won quite easily. This race illustrates the power of the reference class method. Whilst a bettor may be reluctant to place a bet on an unraced horse such as Rosselli, the reference class method provides valuable information relating to race performances of similar runners and in this case shows the horse to be a good betting proposition.

Race Result: *1st Rosselli, 2nd Sammal, 3rd Springs Noblequest*

It is interesting to note that Rosselli went on to win one of the main two-year-old races of the season at Royal Ascot which, in retrospect, made him probably the bet of the year at $6/4$ in this race.

Hamilton 1 June 1998   Going: Good

No	*Cutherbertson & Laird Group Maiden Auction Stakes*			6f

No	Horse	Age and Weight	Trainer	Jockey
1	**Chorus Of Approval**	2 8-12	Miss L A Perratt	Dean McKeown
2	**Pet Express Flyer**	2 8-12	P C Haslam	J Weaver
3	**Dynamic Dancer**	2 8-10	J J O'Neill	W Supple
4	**Rolling Rio**	2 8-9	P C Haslam	J Fortune
5	**Claim Gebal Claim**	2 8-7	Mrs A Swinbank	G Parkin
6	**Gravy Boat**	2 8-7	Miss S E Hall	J Carroll
7	**Red Amazon**	2 8-7	J Berry	G Carter
8	**Pretty Obvious**	2 8-3	R A Fahey	R Winston
9	**Codicil**	2 8-0	Mrs J R Ramsden	N Kennedy
10	**Lady Iona**	2 7-13	Martyn Wane	J McAuley
11	**E B Pearl**	2 7-12	N Bycroft	S Maloney

Starting Prices: 13/8 Pet Express Flyer, 7/2 Dynamic Dancer, 13/2 Red Amazon, 10/1 Chorus Of Approval, 12/1 Pretty Obvious, Rolling Rio, 14/1 Codicil, Gravy Boat, 20/1 Claim Gebal Claim, 50/1 E B Pearl, Lady Iona

Horse Profiles

Horse	RPH	SF	Going	Dist.	Fit	TSR	W-R
Chorus Of Apr'	-	-	✗	✗	✗	2.9	0-0
Pet Express F'	89	31	✗	✗	✓	8.5	0-1
Dynamic Danc'	77	41	✗	✗	✓	4.5	0-2
Rolling Rio	63	62	✗	✗	✓	8.5	0-1
Claim Gebal	32	8	✗	✗	✓	0.0	0-1
Gravy Boat	54	41	✗	✗	✓	12.3	0-1
Red Amazon	76	12	✗	✗	✓	14.6	0-1
Pretty Obvious	84	45	✗	✗	✓	9.5	0-1
Codicil	-	-	✗	✗	✗	4.0	0-0
Lady Iona	-	-	✗	✗	?	9.1	0-0
E B Pearl	58	32	✗	✗	✓	1.6	0-1

Forecast

A very open looking juvenile race, which on form ratings at least is between Pet Express Flyer and Pretty Obvious. However, most of the runners have raced only once or twice and consequently the ratings are very suspect. Only Pet Express Flyer and Dynamic Dancer have previously reached the frame and Red Amazon, from the powerful Jack Berry stable, could only finish ninth on his racecourse debut. The reference class approach produced the following output:

Horse	RC Output	Fair Odds
Chorus Of Apr'	1.5	25/1
Pet Express F'	2.3	16/1
Dynamic Danc'	1.5	25/1
Rolling Rio	2.0	18/1
Claim Gebal	1.5	25/1
Gravy Boat	6.5	5/1
Red Amazon	8.3	7/2
Pretty Obvious	6.9	9/2
Codicil	1.5	25/1
Lady Iona	4.2	8/1
E B Pearl	1.5	25/1

Based on the reference classes, Red Amazon has the best chance of success and is rated a $^7/_2$ prospect. In this respect his starting price of $^{13}/_2$ seemed to offer good value, however he could only finish second to Pet Express Flyer. Both Pretty Obvious and Lady Iona appeared to offer profitable betting opportunities priced at $^{12}/_1$ and $^{50}/_1$ however, they could only finish well beaten in sixth and seventh place respectively.

Race Result: *1st Pet Express Flyer, 2nd Red Amazon, 3rd Claim Gebal Claim*

Epsom 5 June 1998   Going: Good

Vodafone Oaks (Group 1)			**1m 4f**
No Horse	Age and Weight	Trainer	Jockey
1 Bahr	3 9-0	Saeed Bin Suroor	L Dettori
2 Cloud Castle	3 9-0	C E Brittain	J Reid
3 High And Low	3 9-0	B W Hills	D Holland
4 Midnight Line	3 9-0	H R A Cecil	K Fallon
5 Napoleon's Sister	3 9-0	D R C Elsworth	Pat Eddery
6 Shahtoush	3 9-0	A P O'Brien	M J Kinane
7 Tarascon	3 9-0	T Stack	J P Spencer
8 Trophy Wife	3 9-0	H R A Cecil	W Ryan

Starting Prices: 9/4 Midnight Line, 5/2 Bahr, 4/1 High And Low, 8/1 Cloud Castle, 10/1 Napoleon's Sister, 12/1 Shahtoush, Tarascon, 50/1 Trophy Wife

Horse Profiles

Horse	RPH	SF	Going	Dist.	Fit	TSR	W-R
Bahr	124+	88	✓	✗	✓	27.4	3-3
Cloud Castle	128	112	✗	✗	✓	8.6	1-4
High And Low	118	46	✓	✓	✓	12.7	1-2
Midnight Line	127+	103	✓	✗	✓	22.4	4-7
Napoleon's S'	110+	65	✗	✗	✓	10.2	1-2
Shahtoush	128	126	✓	✗	✓	5.3	2-8
Tarascon	123	115	✗	✗	✓	4.2	3-6
Trophy Wife	95	-	✗	✗	✓	22.4	1-11

Forecast

The Oaks is the fillies' equivalent of the Derby and as such is normally contested by many of the best three-year-old middle distance fillies. It would, perhaps, attract even more of the very best fillies if the race was staged on a *fairer* track than Epsom (Epsom's configuration is downhill with a sharp left-hand bend). Based on the form figures many improving animals were entered hence the '+' signs added to the ratings implying that additional improvement could be made, and with five of the runners rated in the 120's it appeared to be an open race. The speed figures, on the other hand, gave Shahtoush an outstanding chance with a rating 11lbs higher than any other horse. All the runners were fit and many had form on the prevailing good going, but only High And Low had proven herself at the distance. The neural network produced the following:

Horse	NN Output	Fair Odds
Bahr	0.12	11/2
Cloud Castle	0.07	18/1
High And Low	0.08	14/1
Midnight Line	0.13	5/1
Napoleon's S'	0.05	25/1
Shahtoush	0.19	11/8
Tarascon	0.05	33/1
Trophy Wife	0.08	14/1

According to the network it was a one horse race, and in fact Shahtoush did surprise many people by winning at $^{12}/_1$. This prediction is the result of the great influence the network places on the speed rating. The two favourites, Bahr and Midnight Line finished second and third and based on the odds generated by the network neither offered a value betting option.

Race Result: *1st Shahtoush, 2nd Bahr, 3rd Midnight Line*

Newmarket 27 June 1998   Going: Good

A & A Electrical Claiming Stakes			1m
No Horse	Age and Weight	Trainer	Jockey
1 Caernarfon Bay	3 9-10	P F I Cole	Pat Eddery
2 The Artful Dodger	3 9-6	R J R Williams	R Cochrane
3 Prodigal Son	3 9-2	R J R Williams	M Hills
4 Broughton Magic	3 8-12	W J Musson	K Fallon
5 Redswan	3 8-12	S C Williams	W Ryan
6 Hoppit	3 8-11	P Howling	O Urbina
7 Leofric	3 8-6	M J Polglase	D Harrison
8 Capercaillie	3 8-4	D Morris	J Tate
9 Elegant Hero	3 8-4	R Hannon	P Fitzsimons
10 Cherished	3 8-3	N Tinkler	R Winston
11 Ferns Memory	3 8-1	W J Musson	A Mackay
12 Shalyah	3 7-13 Mrs J R Ramsden		R Mullen

Starting Prices: 7/4 Shalyah, 5/1 Cherished, Redswan, 8/1 Elegant Hero, 11/1 Leofric, 12/1 Caernarfon Bay, 16/1 Broughton Magic, The Artful Dodger, 33/1 Capercaillie, Hoppit, The Prodigal Son, 50/1 Ferns Memory

Horse Profiles

Horse	RPH	SF	Going	Dist.	Fit	TSR	W-R
Caernarfon Bay	73d	34	✗	✗	✓	12.3	0-5
The Artful D'	57	40	✗	✗	✓	7.0	0-4
Prodigal Son	59	59	✗	✗	✓	7.0	0-7
Broughton M'	53	29	✗	✗	✓	8.9	0-2
Redswan	80	76	✗	✗	✓	14.6	0-4
Hoppit	-	-	✗	✗	✗	4.6	0-0
Leofric	79	79	✓	✗	✓	3.3	0-15
Capercaillie	65	34	✗	✓	✓	9.0	0-7
Elegant Hero	95	77	✗	✗	✓	9.4	0-4

Horse Profiles (continued)

Horse	RPH	SF	Going	Dist.	Fit	TSR	W-R
Cherished	81	71	✓	✓	✓	7.8	1-13
Ferns Memory	49	-	✗	✗	✓	8.9	0-2
Shalyah	84	57	✓	✗	✓	12.4	0-10

Forecast

A very poor race with only one previous winner. In fact, between them, the twelve runners have produced one race win from 68 starts. Based on the form ratings Elegant Hero looks to have a good chance and could improve further since he has only raced twice. Leofric is top rated on time, and is at least suited by the going, however, Cherished is of more interest since she is quite well rated on both form and time and is suited by the distance and the going. The knowledge-based approach produced the following output:

Horse	KBS Output	Odds
Caernarfon Bay	18.2	14/1
The Artful D'	14.0	25/1
Prodigal Son	14.5	20/1
Broughton M'	12.9	28/1
Redswan	20.1	11/1
Hoppit	12.4	28/1
Leofric	25.1	7/1
Capercaillie	20.6	10/1
Elegant Hero	24.1	7/1
Cherished	29.6	9/2
Ferns Memory	12.4	28/1
Shalyah	26.4	6/1

According to the system, this is a very open race and at $^7/_4$ the favourite Shalyah looks to offer extremely poor value. A reasonable price for Cherished is $^9/_2$ and therefore could be backed at the starting price of $^5/_1$.

Race Result: 1st Redswan, 2nd Shaylah, 3rd Cherished

Yarmouth 2 July 1998   Going: Good

Hemsby Conditions Stakes				7f
No Horse	Age and Weight	Trainer		Jockey
1 **Among Men**	4 9-4	M R Stoute		M J Kinane
2 **Igreja**	4 8-13	H R A Cecil		K Fallon
3 **Baltic State**	3 8-3	H R A Cecil		W Ryan
4 **Sottvus**	3 8-3	L M Cumani		G Sparkes

Starting Prices: 3/10 Among Men, 9/2 Igreja, 9/1 Baltic State, 25/1 Sottvus

Horse Profiles

Horse	RPH	SF	Going	Dist.	Fit	TSR	W-R
Among Men	128		✓	✓	✓	17.7	4-7
Igreja	-		✗	✓	?	22.4	2-3
Baltic State	116		✗	✓	?	22.4	2-3
Sottvus	-		✓	✓	✓	17.3	1-2

Forecast

A difficult race for the knowledge base to assess (although the punters found it very easy with a $^3/_{10}$ favourite). The main problem for the system is a lack of information. Igreja was one of the best fillies over a mile in South Africa but has not raced in Europe and consequently has not been rated. Baltic State makes his seasonal debut and Sottvus is also unrated.

Horse	KBS Output	Fair Odds
Among Men	33.0	10/11
Igreja	12.4	11/1
Baltic State	25.2	9/4
Sottvus	12.4	11/1

The knowledge-base selects Among Men as the most likely winner but a starting price of $^3/_{10}$ is far too short compared to the recommended price of $^{10}/_{11}$. Baltic State is the value option.

Race Result: *1st Among Men, 2nd Igreja, 3rd Baltic State*

Newmarket 7 July 1998 Going: Good to firm

No	Horse	Age and Weight	Trainer	Jockey
	Strutt & Parker Maiden Stakes			*7f*
1	**Date**	2 9-0	E A L Dunlop	K Fallon
2	**Gold Lodge**	2 9-0	S C Williams	R Hughes
3	**Learned Friend**	2 9-0	R Hannon	R Cochrane
4	**Meneer**	2 9-0	J H M Gosden	L Dettori
5	**Moutahddee**	2 9-0	M P Tregoning	T Sprake
6	**Nimello**	2 9-0	P F I Cole	T Quinn
7	**Tawwag**	2 9-0	M A Jarvis	P Robinson
8	**Toto Caelo**	2 9-0	B W Hills	M Hills
9	**Waterfront**	2 9-0	P Chapple-Hyam	J Reid

Starting Prices: 6/4 Meneer, 4/1 Tawwag, Waterfront, 7/1 Learned Friend, 8/1 Nimello, 20/1 Toto Caelo, 25/1 Moutahddee, 33/1 Gold Lodge

Horse Profiles

Horse	RPH	SF	Going	Dist.	Fit	TSR	W-R
Date	-	-	✗	✗	?	3.4	0-0
Gold Lodge	-	-	✗	✗	✓	5.4	0-0
Learned Friend	87	45	✗	✗	✓	15.5	0-1
Meneer	91	59	✗	✓	✓	26.0	0-2
Moutahddee	-	-	✗	✗	✗	0.0	0-0
Nimello	-	-	✗	✗	?	16.7	0-0
Tawwag	-	-	✗	✗	✓	7.1	0-0
Toto Caelo	-	-	✗	✗	✓	10.8	0-0
Waterfront	-	-	✗	✗	✓	26.0	0-0

Forecast

A good juvenile maiden with several runners that could have the potential to progress to better races. The two horses with previous experience are rated above average on form but have only produced modest speed figures. Several powerful yards are represented and assessing the most likely winner is a particularly difficult task. The reference class method was applied to the race and the following results generated:

Horse	RC Output	Fair Odds
Date	1.3	80/1
Gold Lodge	6.1	16/1
Learned Friend	9.1	11/1
Meneer	16.8	5/1
Moutahddee	1.3	80/1
Nimello	16.8	5/1
Tawwag	6.1	16/1
Toto Caelo	16.8	5/1
Waterfront	31.3	9/4

Waterfront is selected as the most likely winner and at a starting price of $^5/_1$ is a value bet. The favourite, Meneer, appears under-priced at $^6/_4$, but Nimello and Gold Lodge appear to offer value alternatives at $^8/_1$ and $^{33}/_1$ respectively.

Race Result: *1st Nimello, 2nd Meneer, 3rd Date*

York 10 July 1998   Going: Good to Firm

Stanley Racing Summer Stakes (Listed Race)			6f
No Horse	Age and Weight	Trainer	Jockey
1 **Prends Ca**	5 9-0	W R Muir	J Fortune
2 **Ashraakat**	3 8-12	J L Dunlop	R Hills
3 **Nanoushka**	3 8-12	R Hannon	Pat Eddery
4 **Crazee Mental**	3 8-8	D Haydn Jones	A Mackay
5 **Nadwah**	3 8-8	P T Walwyn	K Darley
6 **Qilin**	3 8-8	M H Tompkins	D Biggs
7 **Vignette**	3 8-8	J H M Gosden	W R Swinburn

Starting Prices: 5/6 Ashraakat, 7/1 Crazee Mental, Qilin, 8/1 Nadwah, Vignette, 9/1 Nanoushka, 33/1 Prends Ca

Horse Profiles

Horse	RPH	SF	Going	Dist.	Fit	TSR	W-R
Prends Ca	97	86	✓	✓	✓	10.6	5-28
Ashraakat	117	106	✓	✓	✓	18.1	2-6

Horse Profiles (continued)

Horse	RPH	SF	Going	Dist.	Fit	TSR	W-R
Nanoushka	110	110	✗	✓	✓	9.4	2-6
Crazee Mental	111	103	✓	✓	✓	11.0	1-10
Nadwah	118d	105	✓	✓	✓	13.1	2-9
Qilin	115	81	✓	✓	✓	10.4	2-7
Vignette	113	77	✓	✓	✓	20.1	1-3

Forecast

A good sprint with all the runners suited by the distance and only Nanoushka doubtful on the good to firm going. Apart from Prends Ca who looks a little outclassed on form, the runners are reasonably well matched. Based on the speed figures, four horses seem to be far superior to the remainder: Nanoushka, Ashraakat, Nadwah, and Crazee Mental. Of these the first two named have most potential for improvement since they have raced the least, and Ashraakat's trainer, John Dunlop, has an outstanding success rate of 18.1% with non-juveniles. It was, therefore, no surprise to see Ashraakat installed as favourite. The neural network generated the following output:

Horse	NN Output	Fair Odds
Prends Ca	0.09	18/1
Ashraakat	0.13	8/1
Nanoushka	0.27	8/11
Crazee Mental	0.11	12/1
Nadwah	0.12	10/1
Qilin	0.09	20/1
Vignette	0.09	18/1

The network generates a very strange prediction, with Nanoushka top rated and given fair odds of $^8/_{11}$. Ashraakat, the favourite, is given odds of $^8/_1$. This can only be due to the emphasis the network places on the speed figures, and hence the prediction looks unreliable.

Race Result: *1st Nanoushka, 2nd Crazee Mental, 3rd Qilin*

Summary

Overall the three systems produced reasonable results for the early part of the 1998 season considering their simplistic form. The knowledge-based approach produced excellent results for pattern races with an average return of 40p per £1 staked. However, the results were not so good for maiden races with the system yielding a loss. This is due to the number of unraced horses contesting maidens, a problem highlighted earlier in the evaluation. Clearly, this would need to be addressed in the final version of the knowledge-base. The reference class approach produced some very interesting results and in general performed quite well. This system may be improved with the addition of other information such as pedigree analyses and foaling dates. The neural network developed in Chapter 7 is too sensitive to changes in the speed figures. Most of the selections are top rated on time making the network totally reliant on one item of data. However, it still produced a profit for the 1998 pattern races analysed although would no doubt benefit from further training on a larger data set.

9

Final Remarks

In recent years the power and capacity of computers has increased rapidly, and in contrast their cost has declined. This, coupled with the availability of horseracing data, has made computer-based selection methods a viable option. At the start of the decade horseracing data was only available in a format suitable for mainframe computers; this has now changed and race data is available on a weekly basis from several suppliers including Raceform and Timeform. As a result the interest in computer-based forecasting techniques for horseracing has grown significantly.

There are two distinct aims of this book. The first is to clearly define the horseracing problem and demonstrate that it can be approached from various perspectives without necessarily requiring the detailed knowledge gained from many years of betting. In fact, once the initial variables have been identified, and a representation established, the problem reduces to a mathematical optimisation task. Consequently, it becomes a problem which can be solved abstractly and is therefore applicable to anyone interested in mathematics, statistics or data modelling. The second aim is to propose, and evaluate various solution methods for the problem. In this text these methods are taken from the field of artificial intelligence however, other disciplines could equally provide techniques for generating workable solutions. It is not an intention of this text to provide the reader with detailed working systems, instead the book illustrates how the proposed methods can be applied by incorporating simple prototype-style systems which can be used to form a basis for more comprehensive solutions.

After providing the necessary background information regarding the horseracing problem, Chapter 3 examined the issue of feature extraction. This is a crucial step in the development of any forecasting system and consequently it is imperative that the correct features are identified and represented in a suitable form for the model. In this particular problem the critical factors on which the models are based are not always directly available, such as the suitability of the race conditions, in which case methods for assessing these factors need to be generated. For example, not all horses possess an ability rating. Whilst this is easily handled by the neural network, it presented the knowledge-based system with a difficult problem and the lack of a rating was, in fact, identified as a severe weakness of the knowledge-based model illustrated in Chapter 6. All of the standard features of the domain have been covered in this text, however, many other features could also have been included. For instance, assessments of pedigrees have not been examined, and this could be especially important for systems applied to juveniles races.

Although there seems to be an endless stream of data for each runner, the information available in the formbook is far less detailed than for American racing with possibly critical data omitted. An additional feature which would improve the success rate of forecasting methods is the weight of each horse; this could be incorporated into a knowledge-base for predicting the likely level of fitness for each runner. However, this is not at present available. Similarly, sectional times (only available for races run at Newmarket) would also assist the assessment of *pace*, a factor considered crucial in American racing.

Of the data that is available, much is subject to varying degrees of uncertainty due to poor measurement techniques employed by the racing officials. For instance, current assessments of the going are very approximate and any improvement in this area would be welcome by race analysts. In addition, the actual race distances are still subject to measurement error with the continual movement of running rails. Race times are also of dubious accuracy at the many courses where hand-timing is still in use. This basic, factual, data is critical for many further calculations and is data which should be 100% reliable, but unfortunately for British race enthusiasts this is not the case.

The first forecasting technique discussed is classified as a rule-based method. In racing this is also referred to as a betting *system*. Systems are very popular in racing since they are easy to operate and can yield very good profits. However, using a system requires a very disciplined approach by the bettor which is especially difficult during long losing runs or if the system continually identifies unfancied horses with low chances of success. Though systems are easy to develop, it is extremely important to check the validity of the methods using either an additional set of test data or the confidence interval technique outlined in Chapter 5, before implementing them.

Knowledge-bases provide the system developer with a framework for constructing detailed programs that consider almost every aspect of the horseracing problem. Due to their form, knowledge-bases can vary in degrees of complexity from very simplistic to extremely detailed. A rapid prototyping approach to development can transform a simple, but fully functional, knowledge-base into a system containing many hundreds of rules representing the complex relationships between the data and a range of concepts. For instance, the ability of a horse can be expressed by the form or speed rating. This would constitute a simple solution. A more comprehensive knowledge-base may consider the number of times the horse has run in order to account for likely improvement, and for unrated horses the trainer's success rate, together with probable starting price and pedigree details. The level of detail in the final knowledge-base, or depth of knowledge, is determined by the knowledge engineer, as well as the complexity of the problem and the availability of domain knowledge, and can be tailored to suit the bettors requirements.

The knowledge-based solution in Chapter 6 uses several different knowledge-bases to evaluate the critical components of an animal's profile, before combining the assessments into a single measure. The system is very simple in form using only three components. This could be viewed as a strength since it requires very little information input by the user, however this simplistic form is the main weakness of the system. When evaluated, the lack of depth in the knowledge, resulting from the omission of other critical data, became apparent and produced selections with fair odds that differed dramatically from the starting prices (see the *New Abbey* race in Chapter 8). However, the knowledge-bases do illustrate how this approach can be applied to the horseracing problem and could be used as the basis of a more complete solution.

The reference class approach is a form of data clustering which compares the profiles of horses with previous race performances to deduce the likely chance of success. Since the profiles need to be generated, this process relies on the output from a set of knowledge-bases designed to evaluate the critical components. The final system, therefore, is a combination of methods. Modifying the approach to improve its forecasting ability can concern amendment to the knowledge-bases in order to produce more accurate profile assessments, an increase in the range of components considered and alternative classification of the factors into classes. Several, or all, of these modifications could be made to the system presented in Chapter 6 in order to generate a more accurate model.

Of all the techniques discussed, the neural network approach is the most interesting. The capability of connectionist systems to *learn* from example cases without any existing domain knowledge is invaluable in the horseracing domain where a large number of historical races is available for evaluation and detailed domain knowledge is difficult to elicit. Furthermore, the ability of the network to uncover previously unknown relationships between the variables may lead to a unique solution which does not follow the standard approaches to forecasting the results of horseraces. Using the network as a data mining tool could generate many previously unconsidered, and profitable, rule-based systems which do not simply mirror the thoughts of the betting public.

Although the simple network presented in Chapter 7 possessed a reasonable degree of forecasting ability, there exists an infinite number of network topologies and a significant proportion of these would no doubt produce better results. In addition, the back-propagation architecture could be replaced with alternative network configurations. For instance, radial basis function networks may more accurately represent the domain. Many texts are available which present the algorithms for these alternative networks and are worth exploring.

Naturally it is possible to combine these symbolic and sub-symbolic approaches into hybrid systems. For instance, the configuration of the knowledge-based neural network is determined by domain knowledge. This is an example of a knowledge-base - neural network hybrid approach. These systems use existing knowledge to define the number of hidden layers, number of hidden nodes and the connections. Clearly, such an approach is applicable to the horseracing problem where some knowledge of solution methods is available. An alternative hybrid using these two technologies involves several neural networks trained to evaluate the critical components before a knowledge-base generates an output rating. The main advantage this would have over a *pure* neural network would be that of explanation. From this architecture it would be possible to generate explanations which justify the conclusions of the system. This additional qualification may be considered important by some users. Genetic algorithms have not been mentioned in this text however they are also applicable. Furthermore a genetic algorithm could be combined with a neural network and used to generate the connections weights as opposed to the network training phase.

In summary, horseracing presents a very challenging problem to the forecaster. It is a particularly well documented domain, offering the researcher a large volume of data with which to work. Interesting characteristics include the level of uncertainty associated with much of the data, the high degree of correlation between many of the predictor variables and the within-race competitive nature of the horseracing process. Horseracing is no longer applicable to just those with a vast knowledge of the subject, the problems it presents are now approachable from abstract perspectives making the problem of interest to bettors and academics alike.

GLOSSARY OF TERMS

All Weather racing refers to races run on an artificial surface, not turf. (See also *Going*)

Backward is a term applied to horses which do not appear to be fully fit. (See also *Looked Well*)

Distance Beaten refers to the distance beaten by another horse and is given in lengths. Normally it applies to the distance a horse is beaten by the winner of a race. (See also *Length*)

Eased is a term used in the *race commentary* to denote horses which are slowed by the jockey in the closing stages of a race.

Exposed horses are those which are unlikely to make dramatic and unexpected improvement. Normally animals which have raced many times. (See also *Unexposed*)

Furlong is a unit of measurement equivalent to $^1/_8$ of a mile.

Form is a general term used to refer to the animal's ability. The phrase 'has shown good form' would indicate that the horse had run well. (See also *Recent Form*)

Going is the term used to denote the ground conditions for turf racecourses. It can range from *Heavy* (very wet, testing ground) to *Hard* (a dry, fast surface) and is categorised as follows: *Heavy, Soft, Good to Soft, Good, Good to Firm, Firm* and *Hard*. (See also *All Weather*)

Group Races represent the most prestigious horseraces in Great Britain. They are sub-divided into three classes (Groups 1, 2 and 3) with winners of Group 1 races receiving the greatest level of prize-money.

Handicap Races are the only events in which horses are artificially handicapped. The weight to be carried by each horse is determined by the

British Horseracing Board's team of handicappers and is based on the animal's previous racecourse performances. These races are intended to give each horse an equal chance of success. (See also *Handicapper*)

Handicapper is used to describe a person who generates handicap ratings (assessments of ability) for horses. Most racing organisations employ one or more handicappers.

Juvenile horses are thoroughbreds aged two years. (See also *Non-juveniles*)

Length is the unit of measurement used to quantify the finishing distances between horses. It equates to the length of a horse at racing pace. (See also *Distance Beaten*)

Listed Races may be considered to be Group 4 events, although unlike Group races some may be handicaps.

Looked Well is a comment applied to horses which look particularly fit and healthy. (See also *Backward*)

Maiden Races are staged for horses which have not previously won a race under Jockey Club rules.

Non-Juvenile horses are thoroughbreds aged three years and upwards. (See also *Juvenile*)

Paddock is an area where the horses parade before racing.

Pattern Races represent the best races staged each year and offer the highest levels of prize-money. (See also *Race Grade*)

Race Commentary refers to a summary of each race performance. This may also contain details of appearance (*paddock* comments) and conformation.

Race Distance is the distance over which the horses race, normally given in miles and furlongs.

Raceform is the organisation which produces the official record of all races and racehorses in Great Britain.

Race Grade identifies the type of race. The *grade* of race will determine, to a certain extent, the ability of the animals taking part and the level of prize-money. (See also *Pattern Races, Maiden Races, Stakes Races* and *Handicaps*)

Race Times are recorded for almost all flat races staged in Great Britain, the majority of which are timed electronically.

Racereader's are employed by most racing organisations, their main task is to generate the *race commentary* and *paddock* comments.

Recent Form refers to the quality of the most recent race performances of a horse.

Stakes Races are non-handicap events which are not specifically classified.

Starting Price's expressed as odds, are associated with every runner and represent the betting public's and bookmakers' opinion of an animal's chances. A price of $^1/_2$ (i.e. two units staked to win one) is considered short, whereas $^{20}/_1$ (i.e. one unit staked to win twenty) is long.

Timeform is a similar organisation to *Raceform*.

Unexposed horses are lightly raced and possess the potential to improve significantly. These horses are often unbeaten. (See also *Exposed*)

APPENDIX A1

Weight-For-Age Table January - Mid July

Dist (f)	Age	Jan 1-31	Feb 1-28	Mar 1-15	Mar 16-31	Apr 1-15	Apr 16-30	May 1-15	May 16-31	Jun 1-15	Jun 16-30	Jul 1-15
5	2	-	-	-	47	44	41	38	36	34	32	30
	3	15	14	13	12	11	10	9	8	7	6	5
6	2	-	-	-	-	-	-	44	41	38	36	33
	3	16	15	14	13	12	11	10	9	8	7	6
7	2	-	-	-	-	-	-	-	-	-	-	38
	3	18	17	16	15	14	13	12	11	10	9	8
8	2	-	-	-	-	-	-	-	-	-	-	-
	3	20	19	18	17	15	14	13	12	11	10	9
9	3	22	21	20	19	17	15	14	13	12	11	10
	4	1	-	-	-	-	-	-	-	-	-	-
10	3	23	22	21	20	19	17	15	14	13	12	11
	4	2	1	-	-	-	-	-	-	-	-	-
11	3	24	23	22	21	20	19	17	15	14	13	12
	4	3	2	1	1	-	-	-	-	1	-	-
12	3	25	24	23	22	21	20	19	17	15	14	13
	4	4	3	2	2	1	1	-	-	-	-	-
13	3	26	25	24	23	22	21	20	19	17	15	14
	4	5	4	3	3	2	1	-	-	-	-	-
14	3	27	26	25	24	23	22	21	20	19	17	15
	4	6	5	4	4	3	2	1	-	-	-	-
15	3	28	27	26	25	24	23	22	21	20	19	17
	4	6	5	4	4	3	3	2	1	-	-	-
16	3	29	28	27	26	25	24	23	22	21	20	19
	4	7	6	5	5	4	4	3	2	1	-	-
18	3	31	30	29	28	27	26	25	24	23	22	21
	4	8	7	6	6	5	5	4	3	2	1	-
20	3	33	32	31	30	29	28	27	26	25	24	23
	4	9	8	7	7	6	6	5	4	3	2	1

The allowances are expressed as the number of pounds that it is deemed the average horse in each age group falls short of full maturity at different race distances over the course of the year.

Weight-For-Age Table Mid July - December

Dist (f)	Age	Jul 15-31	Aug 1-15	Aug 16-31	Sep 1-15	Sep 16-30	Oct 1-15	Oct 16-30	Nov 1-15	Nov 16-30	Dec 1-15	Dec 16-31
5	2	28	26	24	22	20	19	18	17	17	16	16
	3	4	3	2	1	1	-	-	-	-	-	-
6	2	31	28	26	24	22	21	20	19	18	17	17
	3	5	4	3	2	2	1	1	-	-	-	-
7	2	35	32	30	27	25	23	22	21	20	19	19
	3	7	6	5	4	3	2	2	1	1	-	-
8	2	-	37	34	31	28	26	24	23	22	21	20
	3	8	7	6	5	4	3	3	2	2	1	1
9	3	9	8	7	6	5	4	4	3	3	2	2
	4	-	-	-	-	-	-	-	-	-	-	-
10	3	10	9	8	7	6	5	5	4	4	3	3
	4	-	-	-	-	-	-	-	-	-	-	-
11	3	11	10	9	8	7	6	6	5	5	4	4
	4	-	-	-	-	-	-	-	-	-	-	-
12	3	12	11	10	9	8	7	7	6	6	5	5
	4	-	-	-	-	-	-	-	-	-	-	-
13	3	13	12	11	10	9	8	8	7	7	6	6
	4	-	-	-	-	-	-	-	-	-	-	-
14	3	14	13	12	11	10	9	9	8	8	7	7
	4	-	-	-	-	-	-	-	-	-	-	-
15	3	15	14	13	12	11	10	9	8	8	7	7
	4	-	-	-	-	-	-	-	-	-	-	-
16	3	17	15	14	13	12	11	10	9	9	8	8
	4	-	-	-	-	-	-	-	-	-	-	-
18	3	20	18	16	14	13	12	11	10	10	9	9
	4	-	-	-	-	-	-	-	-	-	-	-
20	3	22	20	18	16	14	13	12	11	11	10	10
	4	-	-	-	-	-	-	-	-	-	-	-

The allowances are expressed as the number of pounds that it is deemed the average horse in each age group falls short of full maturity at different race distances over the course of the year.

APPENDIX A2

Trainers' Success Rates for Horses Unraced for 100 Days

| Trainer | Success Rate for all Runners | Horses Unraced for 100 days | | |
		Number of Winners	Number of Runners	Strike Rate
R Akehurst	12.6%	19	218	8.7%
E J Alston	8.4%	2	79	2.5%
D W P Arbuthnot	8.5%	3	57	5.3%
R W Armstrong	14.9%	14	79	17.7%
A Bailey	10.4%	3	86	3.5%
G B Balding	7.8%	5	66	7.6%
I A Balding	12.4%	14	160	8.8%
T D Barron	12.9%	10	91	11.0%
M Bell	12.2%	16	141	11.3%
J Berry	13.4%	20	210	9.5%
J D Bethell	5.8%	4	58	6.9%
M Blanshard	6.8%	0	54	0.0%
S R Bowring	9.7%	4	55	7.3%
J M Bradley	7.0%	1	83	1.2%
J J Bridger	3.1%	0	53	0.0%
C E Brittain	8.1%	13	179	7.3%
M Brittain	7.1%	1	59	1.7%
D Burchell	8.7%	2	60	3.3%
K R Burke	7.7%	2	66	3.0%
N A Callaghan	11.9%	6	51	11.8%
M J Camacho	11.4%	5	71	7.0%
H Candy	9.8%	6	75	8.0%
H R A Cecil	24.9%	37	203	18.2%
Mrs J Cecil	14.3%	14	90	15.6%
M R Channon	10.4%	11	164	6.7%
D W Chapman	8.6%	0	53	0.0%
P W Chapple-Hyam	17.5%	22	151	14.6%
R Charlton	18.8%	23	103	22.3%
P F I Cole	13.9%	36	271	13.3%
H J Collingridge	5.4%	2	58	3.4%
L M Cumani	17.9%	22	133	16.5%
C A Cyzer	8.4%	4	90	4.4%
M Dods	5.4%	2	61	3.3%

Trainer	Success Rate for all Runners	Horses Unraced for 100 days		
		Number of Winners	Number of Runners	Strike Rate
S Dow	7.4%	12	145	8.3%
E A L Dunlop	12.4%	10	66	15.2%
J L Dunlop	17.1%	47	271	17.3%
M H Easterby	8.3%	1	64	1.6%
M W Easterby	7.7%	5	90	5.6%
T D Easterby	9.2%	3	56	5.4%
D R C Elsworth	10.8%	4	95	4.2%
P D Evans	8.9%	2	87	2.3%
J L Eyre	10.4%	8	136	5.9%
J R Fanshawe	11.3%	12	114	10.5%
J G FitzGerald	9.0%	3	60	5.0%
R M Flower	8.7%	1	50	2.0%
J H M Gosden	19.8%	56	236	23.7%
W J Haggas	12.8%	14	67	20.9%
M D Hammond	7.2%	2	93	2.2%
B Hanbury	13.7%	10	77	13.0%
R Hannon	11.3%	34	412	8.3%
J L Harris	7.9%	1	73	1.4%
P W Harris	10.4%	10	120	8.3%
G Harwood	11.0%	6	59	10.2%
P C Haslam	12.0%	6	74	8.1%
D Haydn-Jones	10.3%	2	52	3.8%
M J Heaton-Ellis	8.9%	5	92	5.4%
Lady Herries	14.8%	15	135	11.1%
B W Hills	13.7%	24	214	11.2%
J W Hills	10.1%	13	106	12.3%
R J Hodges	5.9%	2	100	2.0%
R Hollinshead	7.4%	6	119	5.0%
P Howling	4.3%	1	53	1.9%
Lord Huntingdon	14.2%	18	172	10.5%
W Jarvis	11.3%	9	74	12.2%
M A Jarvis	12.3%	3	55	5.5%
J R Jenkins	3.9%	4	80	5.0%
M Johnston	15.3%	20	198	10.1%
Bob Jones	9.7%	7	52	13.5%
A P Jarvis	7.5%	4	71	5.6%
Miss Gay Kelleway	13.7%	17	81	21.0%
G Lewis	11.2%	6	88	6.8%
D R Loder	22.8%	23	119	19.3%
Mrs N Macauley	7.6%	3	54	5.6%

| Trainer | Success Rate for all Runners | Horses Unraced for 100 days | | Strike Rate |
		Number of Winners	Number of Runners	
P J Makin	10.9%	6	108	5.6%
B A Mcmahon	7.9%	4	104	3.8%
B J Meehan	9.9%	6	122	4.9%
A Moore	8.1%	3	55	5.5%
G L Moore	9.6%	5	138	3.6%
G M Moore	8.4%	5	57	8.8%
D Morley	15.7%	7	59	11.9%
W R Muir	9.5%	9	119	7.6%
W J Musson	8.1%	4	79	5.1%
T J Naughton	8.4%	2	85	2.4%
D Nicholls	9.5%	4	119	3.4%
J J O'Neill	4.6%	2	50	4.0%
R J O'Sullivan	11.7%	0	65	0.0%
B Palling	8.2%	5	59	8.5%
J Pearce	10.8%	14	106	13.2%
M C Pipe	13.7%	9	91	9.9%
Sir Mark Prescott	20.5%	19	96	19.8%
Mrs J R Ramsden	11.9%	10	119	8.4%
Mrs M Reveley	13.7%	29	278	10.4%
M J Ryan	10.6%	3	93	3.2%
J L Spearing	8.1%	4	54	7.4%
A C Stewart	15.3%	10	55	18.2%
M R Stoute	17.6%	48	267	18.0%
S Bin Suroor	28.6%	20	80	25.0%
C W Thornton	7.9%	3	77	3.9%
N Tinkler	7.7%	0	81	0.0%
M H Tompkins	9.8%	3	127	2.4%
W G M Turner	8.9%	2	84	2.4%
M D I Usher	5.3%	1	56	1.8%
C F Wall	12.1%	4	64	6.3%
P T Walwyn	12.6%	13	81	16.0%
Martyn Wane	6.2%	1	54	1.9%
J W Watts	9.1%	6	51	11.8%
J Wharton	7.7%	1	58	1.7%
R M Whitaker	6.2%	1	60	1.7%
J White	5.9%	2	73	2.7%
S C Williams	13.3%	7	67	10.4%
S P C Woods	11.7%	8	59	13.6%
G Wragg	16.8%	14	97	14.4%

APPENDIX A3

Back-propagation Algorithm

The algorithm given in this appendix is generally referred to as the back-propagation algorithm and is quite possibly the most popular neural network learning algorithm currently in use. Back-propagation uses a gradient descent approach to minimise some error term with the aim of mapping a set of input patterns to their respective outputs. Training a network by back-propagation involves three stages: the feedforward of the input pattern, the calculation of the error and the back-propagation of the error through the network in the form of weight adjustment. Network interrogation involves only the first of these stages.

In this algorithm it is assumed that the network has only one hidden layer and that the activation is smooth and differentiable.

Algorithm

```
1.    initialise weights
2.    while stopping condition is false do
3.        for each training pattern do
4.            activate input nodes with training pattern
5.            calculate activation of each hidden node
6.            calculate activation of output nodes
7.            calculate weight correction term
8.            calculate bias correction term
9.            for each hidden node sum delta inputs
10.           multiply by derivative of activation
                  function
11.           calculate second weight correction term
12.           calculate second bias correction term
13.           update each weight and bias to output layer
14.           update each weight and bias to hidden layer
          endfor
      endwhile
```

Algorithm Details for Steps 3 to 14

For a network with one hidden layer and one output node:

x	input training vector
target	output target vector
NoInputNodes	number of input nodes
NoHiddenNodes	number of hidden nodes
w	weights from hidden layer to output layer
w[0,j]	bias for *j*th hidden node
v	weights from input layer to hidden layer
v[0]	output node bias
dw	portion of error correction for output layer weights
dw[0]	portion of error correction for output layer bias
dv	portion of error correction for hidden layer weights
dv[0]	portion of error correction for hidden layer biases
h_in	summed contribution to hidden node before activation
a[i]	activation of *i*th hidden node
y_in	summed contribution to output node before activation
y	activation of output node
Activation	the activation function
Derivative	the derivative of the activation function

```
{Steps 4 and 5}
for j:=1 to NoHiddenNodes do
  begin
    h_in[j] := w[0,j];
    for i:=1 to NoInputNodes do
        h_in[j] := h_in[j] + (w[i,j]*x[i]);
    a[j] := Activation(h_in[j])
end;

{Step 6}
y_in := v[0];
for j:=1 to NoHiddenNodes do y_in := y_in + (v[j]*a[j]);
y := Activation(y_in);

{Step 7}
d := (target - y)* Derivative(y_in);
for j:=1 to NoHiddenNodes do dv[j] := alpha*d*a[j];

{Step 8}
dv[0] := alpha*d;
```

{Step 9}
```
for j:=1 to NoHiddenNodes do d_in[j] := d*w[j];
```

{Step 10}
```
for j:=1 to NoHiddenNodes do
    dj[j] := d_in[j]*Derivative(h_in[j]);
```

{Step 11}
```
for j:=1 to NoHiddenNodes do
  for i:=1 to NoInputNodes do
      dv[i,j] := alpha*dj[j]*x[i];
```

{Step 12}
```
for j:=1 to NoHiddenNodes do dv[0,j] := alpha*dj[j];
```

{Step 13}
```
for j:=0 to NoHiddenNodes do w[j] := w[j] + dw[j];
```

{Step 14}
```
for j:=1 to NoHiddenNodes do
    for i:=0 to NoInputNodes do
        w[i,j] := w[i,j] + dv[i,j]
```

APPENDIX A4

Neural Network Simulator - User Guide

The Neural Network Simulator (NNSIM) is a very simple DOS based program which can be used to create, test and interrogate basic feedforward neural networks. It is free to use and distribute. The simulator uses the back-propagation learning algorithm and employs a sigmoid activation function at each hidden and output node. NNSIM allows networks to be defined with up to 20 inputs nodes, 20 hidden nodes and a single output node, with the maximum size of the training file set at 1,000 records.

1. Installation

The neural network simulator can be downloaded from the Web from the following site:

www.raceform.co.uk

Full instructions for downloading and installing the package are given at the site. Briefly, though, the program will run on any PC which supports the DOS operating system. All files are placed in the sub directory C:\NNSIM\ including the training and testing files and the executable file. Whilst the program will run on a 386 machine training times will be very slow and a more powerful machine is recommended. To run the program from windows double-click the nnsim.exe file in program manager, or set up an icon. Running from DOS is simply a matter of typing the file name from the sub-directory.

2. Data Files

Two data files are required for training and interrogating the network:

C:\NNSIM\TRAIN.DAT
C:\NNSIM\INTER.DAT

These files must be present before a network is defined or the system will fail to execute properly. Both files are space delimited ASCII files and can be created using other software such as Microsoft WORD or Excel. The files are organised with one pattern per record. For the training files the first *n* fields of each record refer to the inputs with the final field the target output. An example of the training file is given in figure 1. For the interrogation file the target output is not known and can be substituted with a zero.

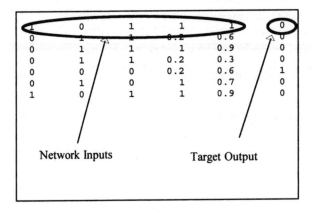

1	0	1	1	1	0
0	1	1	0.2	0.6	0
0	1	1	1	0.9	0
0	1	1	0.2	0.3	0
0	0	0	0.2	0.6	1
0	1	0	1	0.7	0
1	0	1	1	0.9	0

Network Inputs   Target Output

Figure 1: Training file example

As mentioned in Chapter 7 the data presented to a feedforward network needs to be normalised and this is the case for NNSIM. If the simulator detects a data item which does not lie in the [0,1] range it will terminate execution.

Four other data files are created by the simulator:

        C:\NNSIM\WEIGHTS.ANN
        C:\NNSIM\WEIGHTS.BAK
        C:\NNSIM\ERRORS.DAT
        C:\NNSIM\RESULTS.INT

C:\NNSIM\WEIGHTS.ANN holds the numeric weights of the network and is modified during the training phase. This file is discussed in more detail in section 6. A backup of this file (WEIGHTS.BAK) is made on each new run of the program to provide extra security. The *errors* file simply records the mean squared error of the network and can be examined to monitor the performance of training.   The *results* file stores the output of network interrogations and is discussed in section 5.

3. Creating a Network

The first step in developing a network is defining the network structure. NNSIM allows two options, the first is to create a completely new network, and the second is to continue training an existing network.

```
+=============================================================+
|                                                             |
|         ARTIFICIAL NEURAL NETWORK SIMULATOR                 |
|                                                             |
|  D - define network structure    R - randomise weights      |
|                                                             |
|  T - train network               I - interrogate network    |
|                                                             |
|  S - save trained network        C - check training data    |
|                                                             |
|                    Q - quit system                          |
|                                                             |
|  Enter a selection >>>                                       |
|                                                             |
+=============================================================+
```

Figure 2: Menu options for NNSIM

Both options are covered by the *define network structure* choice on the NNSIM menu (illustrated in figure 2). Once the *define* option is selected the user can choose between training an existing network or defining a new structure.   Using an existing file allows training to continue on a partially trained network, or the architecture to be used for training a new network in which case the network weights should be randomised before training commences. If a new network is required the user needs to input the number of input and hidden nodes, together with the learning rate. The number of input and hidden nodes must not exceed 20 in each case and the learning rate should be between 0 and 1. A high learning rate may allow the network to train faster but is more likely to reach a local minimum whereas a low learning will train slower but is more likely to reach the global minimum. As a guide use a figure between 0.1 and 0.5.

Once the network structure is defined (either existing or new) the data files are checked for errors; if any invalid inputs are found the simulator will terminate. These invalid data items will need to be corrected before the simulator is re-run.

4. Training/Testing a Network

Once the network has been defined and the files validated, the network can be trained. For *new* networks or for networks which are to be retrained, it is important to randomise the weights before training. Neural networks can be sensitive to the initial weights so it is very important to use this randomise procedure. After randomising the weights it is simply a matter of choosing the train option to start network training. The following screen (figure 3) will be displayed.

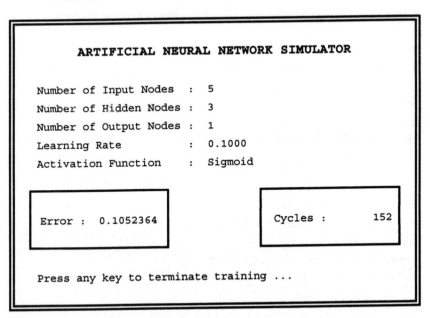

```
        ARTIFICIAL NEURAL NETWORK SIMULATOR


    Number of Input Nodes   :   5
    Number of Hidden Nodes  :   3
    Number of Output Nodes  :   1
    Learning Rate           :   0.1000
    Activation Function     :   Sigmoid


    Error :   0.1052364              Cycles :        152


    Press any key to terminate training ...
```

Figure 3: Training screen

The training screen, illustrated in figure 3, is divided into three distinct parts. The top section of the screen presents the architecture of the network, in the example the network has five input nodes, three hidden nodes and one output node; the learning rate is set at 0.1 and the activation function is sigmoid. The second part of the screen concerns the error. This is updated every 10 cycles and shows how well the network is converging. Ideally this value will continue to decrease until the global minimum has been located. This error is also written to the *error* file for further examination. The final part of the screen is the cycles box. This updates after every cycle and shows how many times the training file has been examined by the network.

Training can be terminated at any time by pressing any key and can be resumed by choosing the train option from the main menu. To test how well the network is representing the training patterns the *check option* in the main menu can be invoked. This simply presents a screen showing the number of training patterns, the number correctly classified and the ratio of correctly classified training patterns subject to a tolerance level of 0.1.

A trained network can also be saved from the main menu (option *S*) if training is to be suspended or the network has found a usable solution.

5. Interrogating a Network

Interrogation, in this instance, simply means testing the network on new data patterns. The interrogation file C:\NNSIM\INTER.DAT holds the new patterns in the same format as the training file. Selecting the interrogation option from the main menu instructs the network to examine each of these new records and output to the *results* file the record together with the network's output.

A section of the results file is shown in figure 4. The input pattern is shown to the left of the file with the network's output on the right. It should be remembered that the network output is normalised to the [0,1] range, and therefore an amount of post-processing may be required to convert the output to a standard form.

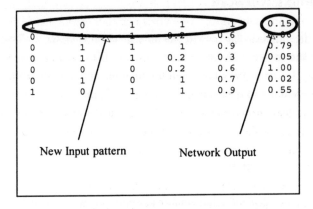

	0	1	1	1	0.15
0	1	1	0.2	0.6	1.00
0	1	1	1	0.9	0.79
0	1	1	0.2	0.3	0.05
0	0	0	0.2	0.6	1.00
0	1	0	1	0.7	0.02
1	0	1	1	0.9	0.55

New Input pattern   Network Output

Figure 4: A section of the results file

6. The Weights File

Once trained and tested it may be desirable to locate the network in another software package. To facilitate this the weights file has been provided in an easy to read format.

The first three lines of the weights file show the number of input nodes, the number of hidden nodes and the learning rate. (This learning rate can be changed during training by adjusting the value in this file before resuming training). The first group of weights (the W weights) refer to the weights from the hidden layer to the output node. Weight $W0$ is the weight from the bias, $W1$ from the first hidden node, $W2$ from the second hidden node etc. The V weights refer to the weights from the input layer to the hidden layer and are ordered according to the input nodes. Therefore, all weights from the first input node are listed first, followed by the second input node and so on. The notation shows the input node number followed by the hidden layer node number. For instance, $V12$ would imply the weight from the first input node to the second hidden node and $V03$ denotes the weight from the bias to the third hidden node. Each block of V weights starts with a *dummy* weight which plays no part in the network structure. These values normally contain several zeros and simply act as a divider between the input node weights. Consequently, if the network function was to be transferred to another program these dummy weights could be ignored. At the end of the weights list the number of completed cycles is given.

7. Example Network

The data files include the second example given in Chapter 7. There are 13 training patterns and 21 test vectors in the files *train.dat* and *inter.dat* respectively. These files can be used to train and test different network architectures; the example quoted in Chapter 7 uses a 1-12-1 network but changing the number of hidden nodes may result in more efficient training.

8. Other Software

There is a great deal of other neural network software available from the internet. Although many commercial systems can be purchased, there are also freeware and shareware packages available, some of which are very comprehensive and allow large networks to be constructed. NNSIM is only intended to give a brief overview of developing an artificial neural network, and users who wish to develop more detailed networks should first test these other packages.

APPENDIX A5

Results of Rule-Based Methods for 1998

This section presents a summary of the results of the rule-based methods proposed in Chapter 5 for the 1998 turf season. The summary includes all races up to 18 July 1998.

Method 1: Juvenile Favourites

Rule 1

Date	Horse	Starting Price	Finishing Position
16 June	Bertolini	6/1	5th
20 June	Spirit Willing	7/2	WON
6 July	Baltic Lowland	10/11	3rd
7 July	Spirit Willing	13/8	5th
8 July	Bertolini	3/1	WON
12 July	Charmes	7/2	WON

Rule 2

Date	Horse	Starting Price	Finishing Position
13 May	Red Sea	3/1	WON
20 June	Spirit Willing	7/2	WON
8 July	Compatriot	12/1	4th
9 July	Choirgirl	9/2	4th

Summary: 5 winners from 10 bets (50%); average return per £1: 115p.

Method 2: 100% Success Method

Date	Horse	Starting Price	Finishing Position
14 March	Diamond Flame	13/8	WON
2 April	Tajasur	4/9	2nd
11 April	Benin	3/1	4th
14 April	Daring Derek	8/15	WON
14 April	Mister Rambo	2/1	2nd
16 April	Border Arrow	11/4	WON
16 April	Himself	10/1	6th
18 April	Soviet Bureau	4/1	4th
21 April	High-Rise	2/1	WON
28 April	Sadian	6/4	WON
2 May	The Sandfly	5/1	7th
2 May	Touchez Du Bois	16/1	5th
3 May	Merciless	5/1	8th
4 May	Asad	5/6	WON
5 May	Seignorial	20/1	5th
8 May	Charlies Bride	7/2	2nd
8 May	Colours To Gold	11/1	12th
10 May	Amenixa	14/1	5th
15 May	Abyaan	7/2	5th
15 May	Gorse	5/6	2nd
15 May	Sultana	10/1	4th
21 May	Digitalize	Evens	WON
23 May	Deep Dive	7/1	2nd
23 May	Talavera	7/1	9th
25 May	Casino Captive	4/5	WON
3 June	Eaton Square	Evens	WON
6 June	Royal Anthem	4/9	WON
8 June	Godabi	2/1	6th
8 June	Second Wind	11/1	5th
11 June	Zante	7/4	2nd
24 June	Pure Gold	12/1	4th
4 July	Catchascatchcan	8/1	WON
4 July	Dark Shell	7/1	6th
4 July	Nedawi	7/4	3rd
10 July	Dushanbe	2/1	3rd

Date	Horse	Starting Price	Finishing Position
10 July	White Heart	13/8	WON
10 July	Dushanbe	2/1	3rd
10 July	White Heart	13/8	WON
17 July	Innuendo	5/4	WON

Summary: 13 winners from 37 bets (35%); average return per £1: -1.8p.

Method 3: The Draw

Date	Track	Draw (Rns)	Starting Price	Finishing Position
1 May	Musselburgh	1 (17)	14/1	3rd
1 May	Musselburgh	2 (17)	16/1	11th
6 May	Musselburgh	1 (8)	3/1	2nd
6 May	Musselburgh	2 (8)	7/4	WON
12 May	York	1 (11)	14/1	11th
12 May	York	2 (11)	11/2	WON
13 May	York	1 (9)	13/2	9th
13 May	York	2 (9)	10/1	7th
14 May	York	1 (16)	20/1	14th
14 May	York	2 (16)	6/1	WON
14 May	York	1 (13)	11/2	2nd
14 May	York	2 (13)	7/1	WON
15 May	Hamilton	8 (10)	25/1	5th
15 May	Hamilton	9 (10)	50/1	2nd
15 May	Hamilton	10 (10)	20/1	6th
1 June	Hamilton	16 (18)	50/1	13th
1 June	Hamilton	17 (18)	7/1	5th
1 June	Hamilton	18 (18)	14/1	9th
5 June	Epsom	1 (14)	11/4	13th
5 June	Epsom	2 (14)	25/1	9th
3 July	Hamilton	12 (14)	12/1	6th
3 July	Hamilton	13 (14)	12/1	4th
3 July	Hamilton	14 (14)	6/1	2nd
6 July	Musselburgh	1 (16)	14/1	6th
6 July	Musselburgh	2 (16)	33/1	11th
			Starting	Finishing

Date	Track	Draw (Rns)	Price	Position
10 July	Hamilton	12 (14)	50/1	11th
10 July	Hamilton	13 (14)	14/1	7th
10 July	Hamilton	14 (14)	9/1	WON
10 July	York	1 (12)	16/1	3rd
10 July	York	2 (12)	7/1	5th
11 July	York	1 (20)	12/1	6th
11 July	York	2 (20)	33/1	pulled up
15 July	Sandown	10 (11)	9/2	WON
15 July	Sandown	11 (11)	5/1	4th

Summary: 6 winners from 34 bets (18%); average return per £1: 17p

INDEX